The Money-Saving Idea Book:

Inside Tips for Starving Students,

Frugal Seniors and Every

Financial Survivor

Copyright 2009

Ed Creager

Foreword

This book is a collection of money-saving ideas designed to help you make your resources "work harder" for you. Many ideas involve new ways of doing things, and no one is likely to use every idea offered here. Also, an idea that might seem silly or obvious *to you* might be helpful to someone else. So, it's important to note that each reader can and should choose which ideas fit their interests and needs, and the <u>extensive index</u> will be helpful to many readers in finding these ideas.

Note that the book includes "Idea Numbers," <u>but not page numbers</u>. Having two numbering systems would have been confusing.

The Table of Contents provides a general overview of the book. The final chapter ("Other / Multiple Topics") might be the most useful one for some readers as it contains the greatest percentage of ideas that people are unlikely to have encountered elsewhere. Note that although ideas relating to cable/satellite television could have been placed in "Utilities," they were placed in "Information and Entertainment" where they seemed to fit equally well.

Be sure to see the nine topics listed in the index under "major savings techniques." Readers who give these areas special attention are likely to get the greatest benefit from this book.

Some of the ideas presented here are quite simple, and some are more complicated and are therefore described in greater detail. Some ideas might appeal to nearly everyone, and some ideas are only for the most frugal people.

Please also note that, for most of the topics addressed here, the money-saving ideas are not intended to *completely* cover a given topic. While the ideas relate to a wide range of money-saving techniques, there are plenty of additional sources of information about financial topics, including the internet, libraries and other governmental sources.

The point of this guidebook is to offer options for saving money, *not* to preach or cause doubt or worry. <u>In short, take what you like and leave the rest -- just like you would at a salad bar</u>.

Some of the most important ideas and themes of this book are <u>underlined</u>. After reading this book, an excellent method for reviewing and reinforcing what you've read is to scan through for and re-read the underlined items.

Note that all websites mentioned herein, and any associated trademarks and/or service marks are the property of their respective owners. Being listed in this book does not imply endorsement by the author nor by the publisher. They are not affiliated with, nor owned by, the author of this book, except for the author's personal website which can be visited at:

http://www.edcreager.blogspot.com

… please take a look at the other publications <u>and discounts</u> that are available at the website.

Finally, some ideas involve spending a little in order to save a lot, so allow time (sometimes a month or two) for money that you save to start showing up in your wallet or bank account.

Disclaimer

The resources provided, including websites, books and related materials, are intended to provide accurate information regarding the subject matter. All products and services are provided with the understanding that neither the author nor the publisher is engaged in rendering legal, accounting, or other professional advice. If expert assistance is needed, the services of a competent professional person (such as a lawyer, accountant, etc.) should be sought.

Both the author and publisher specifically disclaim any responsibility for any loss, liability or risk, personal or otherwise, which is incurred as a direct or indirect consequence of the use or application of any of this book's contents.

Table of Contents

Chapter #	Chapter Topics	Begins with Idea No.
1.	**Banking and Finances**.. Includes bank and credit card accounts and statements, interest charges and debit cards.	1
2.	**General Shopping and Spending**.................... Includes food and beverages, along with other routine purchases.	19
3.	**Household Items and Services**........................ Includes clothing, dishes, flatware, greeting cards and gifts.	87
4.	**Housing Costs**.. Includes rent, mortgage loans and refinancing.	141
5.	**Information and Entertainment**........................ Includes books, education, television, computer and the internet.	147
6.	**Travel and Vacations**... Includes routine travel as well as tourism, safe driving information and public transportation.	159
7.	**Utilities**.. Includes electricity, telephones, water, lighting and appliances.	173
8.	**Vehicles**... Includes purchases and maintenance, insurance, etc.	205
9.	**Other / Multiple Topics**..................................... Includes items that don't fit into another category or that involve multiple topics.	217

Banking and Finances

1. Keep money "in the family." For example, if you have a broken chair, and a family member or close friend can do a good job fixing furniture, consider asking them to fix it for free or for a very low fee. They might return the favor. In any case, there will be more money kept within your "inner circle".

2. Make yourself "get up and go" buy an item when the time is definitely right. <u>Motivate yourself to save money</u>. **However, <u>very rarely</u> is it a good idea for consumers to borrow money.** In fact, one of the most effective ways to save money is to pay off any outstanding loans and debts (including credit card balances) that cost you money in the form of interest.

If you owe money, you should regularly review credit card statements (and any other loan documents) that show

how much interest you are paying. Many times, the true rate of interest, and the dollar amounts of interest and other fees appear in small print, often on the backs of these statements! Take a little time to be sure you understand how much you're paying, and remember that <u>paying interest means that you're spending money to rent money</u>!

3. <u>If you use a credit card, compare it to others that are available</u>. **Shop for the best interest rate and be wary of temporarily low rates that are adjusted upwards after a few months.** Also, most people with a good credit rating can get a card with no annual fee. If you often carry a balance on at least one card, you might want to call one or more credit card companies and ask them to reduce your interest rate. If they won't, you have the option of closing that account after finding a better card.

4. Every month, pay off the balance on your credit card(s), if you can. Credit cards *carry very high interest rates* compared to nearly any other type of loan. And remember that any outstanding balance from month to month is a loan that you are "carrying" and therefore paying interest on.

5. Avoid having too many credit cards. Many people have only one card – usually one of the widely-accepted cards. Having only one, or perhaps two cards, tends to reduce any fees you pay. It also makes it easier to keep track of how much money you owe, and when payments are due. **Also, many people tend to spend (and therefore borrow) more if they have more than one or two credit cards.**

6. If you tend to spend too much during the holidays, you might save up money beforehand, and then pay for gifts using cash only. Just try it for one holiday season. You'll reduce your interest expenses and likely be in better financial shape when January rolls around.

7. Use a checking account that has low monthly charges (if any) and if possible, pays interest. (Note that the interest-bearing checking account is, in many places, a "thing of the past," but if you can get one, it's a great option unless it's an account with fees that will cancel out your interest.) If the account requires a minimum balance to avoid a service charge or to earn interest, try to maintain the necessary minimum balance whenever you can.

If you have trouble doing this, you might want to look for an account at a bank that offers choices that better suit you. Different banks offer a wide variety of options, so shop around. Note that it's often wise to have more than one type of account (checking and savings for example) at a given bank so that you're eligible for certain discounts, etc.

Make a point of keeping enough money in a checking (or similar) account to meet your regular expenses without falling below any minimum balance; and you should probably allow a little more money in addition to this total as a "cushion" against falling below the minimum. Otherwise, you risk incurring fees that can be substantial, or, by some estimations, outrageous.

Consider your options carefully before switching banks or moving an account from one bank to another. But if your current bank fails to meet your needs or consistently charges you fees for routine services, don't hesitate to switch banks after you locate a better deal.

(Note that like many other topics covered in this guidebook, banking services are a very personal matter.

For example, some people prefer to choose a bank based on the convenience of its branches or its level of service rather than being concerned primarily with fees and expenses. As always, do what seems right for you, even if this means not changing a thing!)

8. <u>Don't leave too much money in a checking account</u>. Any money you have in a checking account that's in excess of any required minimum (plus regular expenses and a "cushion"... see idea #7) can almost always earn a higher rate of interest in another type of account such as a savings or money market account. **Why leave any substantial amount of money where it will earn little or no interest?**

Reasons to have a savings account or money market account include: to deal with emergencies and unexpected expenses, to earn interest, and to save up for major items like a car, a down payment on a home, education, etc. But remember that having money in your savings account shouldn't be used as an excuse to overspend from your checking account. In other words, **having money isn't a reason to spend money**.

9. <u>If you have one or more automatic teller machine (ATM) cards, be sure you are aware of any fees that you pay</u>. Some people are unaware that banks charge as much as $4.00 or more when the card is used anywhere besides one of their bank's ATMs. Even using a card at one of your own bank's machines can incur a substantial fee. If you're regularly incurring ATM fees, you might want to ask yourself: "Why should I have to pay to get my own money back?"

Consider that cashing a check at a teller window usually costs only whatever you pay for the actual check -- often less than ten cents. Some banks charge a per-check charge, but this is usually very low compared to the cost of using a card. (Note that some banks charge a substantial fee for check-cashing if you don't have an account at their bank.)

10. Be wary of investment opportunities and major purchases until you're sure you understand your options and can make decisions based on information from sources you trust.

11. Save your credit card receipts, at least until your bill arrives. Then, look at your credit card bills carefully to be sure you have not been double-billed or otherwise overcharged. Also, save receipts (or copies of them, depending on your filing methods) for items that might be tax deductible. All of this also applies if you make purchases with a debit card, except that you'll of course compare those receipts to your bank statement.

12. <u>Keep your financial records in order</u>, especially tax records. Having all of your receipts and other financial records arranged so that you can find them at tax time can save you a lot of time, and can help you qualify for tax deductions you might otherwise lose.

13. You might want to be extremely wary of so-called "bill consolidation loans" and similar loans. Often, their interest rates are much higher than those of other loans that might be available to you. Also, if you own your home (with or without a typical or "first" mortgage), note that at least a few of those people who lend money based on a home's value would like nothing better than to foreclose on your home. For those who don't know it already, there are "sharks" in this world who will do nearly anything for financial gain. They will take from you whatever they can get, including your home. None of this in intended to make you afraid, but rather to make you aware of how important it is to understand *any* loan

<u>before signing loan documents</u>. Being informed helps keep people out of trouble.

To review: Avoid borrowing against the value of your home if you can. If you decide to borrow money based on the value of your home, be very careful that you understand the terms of the loan (second mortgage, home equity, etc.) Falling behind on payments with this kind of loan can be very expensive. In the worst case, you could lose your home.

14. <u>Avoid borrowing money</u>. With rare exceptions (such as the purchase of a home which often has major tax advantages), most people rarely *need* to borrow money. Interest on loans is an expense that can be avoided with a little common sense and self-restraint. If you still owe money on your vehicle, consider driving the vehicle for a few years after the loan has been paid off, while you save money that you can put toward buying your next vehicle outright, i.e., with no loan. If you can't pay for it outright, you can at least reduce your loan payments by making a large down payment. If you don't have a vehicle loan, try to keep it that way. **Remember that paying interest is paying to "rent money."**

15. Consider buying checks for your checking account directly from a company that prints them rather than through your bank. Offers from check printers sometimes appear along with coupons that arrive in the mail or in Sunday newspapers. Alternatively, you can find suppliers online by searching on "new checks". These special offers are often better than the fees charged by your local bank.

16. Consider using automatic, direct payments from a checking account to pay routine bills and/or using "direct deposit" for paychecks. Each of these methods can help you reduce travel, saving both time and money. By paying bills this way, you can also save on postage.

17. If you have trouble controlling your spending because it's so easy to spend using a credit card, consider getting a debit card instead. Some people have saved thousands of dollars over time by taking this perhaps drastic step. As an alternative, you might want to keep a single card for true emergencies, but keep it in a safe place other than your wallet/purse.

18. Look at every bank statement you receive to be sure there are no charges you haven't authorized. Sometimes your bank might charge a fee because your balance has fallen below a certain level – a "minimum balance." In addition, they often have the right (often disclosed only in your initial account agreement) to change the minimum balance at any time. Unless you keep an eye open for charges like this, you could end up paying them repeatedly without realizing it.

General Shopping and Spending

19. Use a method called the "Three Cs" before you leave the house to do any significant shopping. The three words to remember are "<u>comparison</u>", "<u>checklist</u>" and "<u>coupons</u>". In other words, have you <u>compared</u> products and/or looked through sales circulars/catalogs to find the best prices? Have you made a written <u>checklist</u> that corresponds to which stores you'll visit and what items you plan to buy? (This can save you a lot by reducing mileage and eliminating unneed trips.) Finally, have you clipped any relevant coupons and remembered to take them with you?

20. <u>Stock up when items you really need are on sale</u>. For smaller items that don't spoil quickly (like detergent, shampoo and toothpaste), watch for a price which is especially low. **Then, buy a supply that will last for**

several months, or on certain items, and depending on your budget, buy enough to last for a year or more. (Bear in mind that some items are sensitive to temperature, humidity, etc., so they could deteriorate while in storage.)

21. <u>Buy and eat pasta</u>. It is cheap, relatively nutritious, can be stored for long periods, and can be used in many kinds of recipes. Note that thin types of pasta such as "angel hair" pasta cook faster than thicker varieties. Choosing thin varieties of pasta will help you to save time and reduce your utility costs by a small amount.

22. <u>"Impulse buying" should be avoided as much as possible</u>. In other words, plan your shopping, and then buy only what you intended to buy. More specifically, be sure to avoid the high mark-up items that retailers put on display near their cash registers. They usually know which types of items represent tempting, last-minute

purchases, and nearly all of them purposely display these items where you will see them while you wait in line.

23. If you buy cigarettes, consider buying them by the carton. Better yet, find a discount store (if your state allows them) and buy more than one carton at a time when they're on sale. (At the risk of sounding preachy, it must be said that it's much better to not smoke at all. There are many reasons for this, of course, including the positive effects that not smoking has on a person's health as well as on one's finances.)

24. <u>Try not to pay for convenience</u>. Example: don't pay more per gallon for gasoline simply to avoid driving a few blocks farther.

25. <u>Pay particular attention to unit pricing</u>. For example, one pound of peanuts for $1.35 is better than ten ounces for $1.19. (The unit prices are 8.4 cents per ounce and 11.9 cents per ounce, respectively.)

26. <u>Avoid going to the grocery store when you're hungry</u>, because you're more likely to buy more than a sensible amount of food. Hungry shoppers also are likely to buy more expensive items (like single-serve snacks) that are featured in some stores.

27. Whenever practical, buy items featured at "loss leader" or "half-price" sale events. A loss leader sale is a method used by retailers to get customers to come into their stores so they will purchase several more items. Typically, a popular loss leader item is sold at or even below the store's cost for that item.

28. <u>Buy large amounts of an item and split the cost</u> with a friend, neighbor or roommate. Example: Buy a 40-pound bag of dog food and divide it up into smaller bags or pails... then "settle up" with the other person.

(For this idea to be effective, the purchase of a large amount would need to represent a substantial per-unit savings based on the large quantity being purchased.)

29. When looking for information about a product, many people <u>trust the opinions and information in magazines that don't accept advertising</u>. This reduces the likelihood of biased reporting in favor of a magazine's advertisers.

30. Make your own salads rather that buying from a salad bar. Many salad bar ingredients cost less than $2.00/lb. when purchased individually. Salad bars, although they offer convenience, often are priced at over $4.00/lb. This is another example of the idea that you should <u>try not to pay for convenience</u>.

31. Don't buy too much of an item. If a product will be useful five years from now, it's smart to buy a large amount of it when it's on sale, but don't buy so much fresh produce (for example) that some of it will spoil.

32. Unless you really need a particular kind of service, don't pay for it. A good example of putting this idea in effect is to eat at "self service" restaurants. Some restaurants -- even some upscale establishments -- are designed so that you pick up your meal at a counter or steam table and then seat yourself, which eliminates the custom of tipping. Another food-related idea is to reduce how often you eat in restaurants by trading off "cooking nights" with neighbors. Each week, for example, they make a meal for your family on one night of the week, and on another night, you make a meal for theirs. Each family gets a prepared meal and no one pays for table service.

33. Except for loss leaders, <u>reduce your purchases of prepared foods</u>. Foods that have had little or no processing are almost always cheaper than prepared foods, and often are healthier too. (Note: the term "loss leader" is defined along with idea number 2, above.)

34. Try to plan for all kinds of expenses, so that you avoid fines, late fees, etc. (Remember that when you pay these fees, you get nothing tangible in return for your money!) In order to plan for future expenses, you might, for example, set aside a few minutes on the first Saturday of every month to consider what expenses you can expect in the next few months. Then, if necessary, move money from one kind of account to another, cash out an investment, or, if possible, reduce another expense so that you'll have the needed funds.

One excellent tool (and to some people an obvious one) for planning and managing your money is a budget. Computer software is available for use in creating and maintaining a budget. Also, many libraries have information on how to prepare a budget.

35. Some cooks can avoid buying any kind of gravy mix. Instead, they can use juices from meat products to make their own gravy. Fully cooked meat juices can be frozen for later use.

36. When you eat at a restaurant, <u>look for group/family deals</u> that provide a complete meal for several people at one reasonable price. Often, <u>daily "specials"</u> also can save you a lot of money.

37. You might want to <u>try to eliminate or reduce costly habits like coffee drinking and cigarette smoking</u>. If you drink a lot of coffee, consider switching to tea; it's cheaper than coffee in almost all places. Also, plain water and ice water are available at virtually no cost.

38. <u>Use manufacturers' coupons</u>, but (1) only on items you would consider buying even without a coupon, and

(2) only if your final cost using a coupon is less than all store brands and generic products that are acceptable to you.

Often, the final cost of a "store brand" product without a coupon will be less than a "name brand" product with a coupon. <u>You can save a lot when a store brand product is offered at a sale price</u>.

Note: offers that require you to purchase several items in order to receive a discount or a "free" item, often are *not* the best available deals. As an example, an offer that requires you to buy two bottles of cola to receive a "free" bag of snacks is likely to involve your paying too much for the cola in order to receive an overpriced name brand snack.

39. Cooking a roast can be a money-saving opportunity! Try to buy a lean roast when it's on sale.

(Leaner meat means that less of your money is spent on fat, much of which ends up in the bottom of the pan after cooking.) Then, add <u>plenty</u> of the kinds of vegetables that are inexpensive in your area... they're likely to be items such as potatoes, carrots, and onions, which, although they are usually very cheap, are still enjoyed by most people. (Vary these instructions according to your tastes, of course, by selecting additional vegetables and adding any spices that you like.)

40. If you can find the time (or "make" the time) to prepare homemade biscuits and/or cookies, they are real money savers compared to the store-bought versions.

41. Bananas that are about to spoil can be frozen and used later in specific recipes for items like banana bread, pudding, etc.

42. When you use coupons, try to use them at stores

that give you credit for double the coupon's face value.

43. At restaurants, <u>consider asking for ice water</u>, which usually is free or nearly free. At restaurants that offer "take-out" service, consider buying only food (no drink) and eating it at home... then you can drink whatever you've already bought at a "grocery store price" instead of a "restaurant price."

44. <u>Avoid paying for advertising</u>. Consider which suppliers of an item seem to do the most advertising. Often, these will be the *most expensive* suppliers. Buying store brands and shopping at discount stores are often good choices in this regard.

45. If you don't do it already, <u>consider planning some of your meals around fish instead of other meats</u>. Tuna and several other kinds of fish are relatively inexpensive, and are nutritious, flavorful, high in protein, and useful in many different recipes. Tuna and other kinds of fish are low in fat, and some fish contains fat that is relatively good for you when eaten in reasonable amounts. **Note that some people have food allergies or other health concerns that should be considered before making dietary changes.**

46. You might want to buy fruit juices in the form of concentrate rather than buying the usually higher-priced varieties that are often sold in bottles or cartons.

47. When making beverages from a powder or from concentrated juice, try adding a bit of extra water. For example, where three cans of water are called for, use three-and-a-half cans instead. **This technique is equivalent to paying about 12% less for the product.**

48. If you buy instant tea, consider instead buying teabags or ordinary ground tea leaves. Often, they are much less expensive than instant tea. Coffee that you brew yourself is likewise cheaper (in most cases) than instant coffee.

49. If you live with a person who has a tendency to overeat, try to discretely arrange for another person to do most of the food shopping. You likely will save money and you might be doing the overeater a favor, too.

50. If you buy packaged side dishes, consider returning to some simpler foods that were more popular in the past. The preparation of some very basic side dishes is not time-consuming. One possible choice is potatoes (baked, boiled, etc.), which are inexpensive and don't take much effort to prepare. Many other kinds of vegetables also can be prepared by simply boiling them for a short time and adding any seasoning, butter, etc., that you like.

51. Leave the skin on potatoes, unless you don't enjoy eating the outer layer, which is the most nutritious part. You'll be getting more food for your money.

52. Here are three strategies for routine shopping:

(1) If you have good "puzzle-solving" skills, prepare a master list of the grocery and household items that you use most often. Then plan a single shopping trip once each week or so, and arrange the master list to match a good route from store to store. You'll save time and you'll save money on gas, too. Over time, as you <u>stock up</u> on things you need and eliminate unneeded items from your list, you'll be able to reduce your travel and purchases.

(2) Get a Sunday newspaper <u>and save coupons for items you *might* buy</u>. Keep each week's coupons together in a group. This makes it easier to discard unused coupons if they expire.

(3) <u>Save the grocery store insert(s)</u> from the Sunday newspaper until the end of each sale period. Then, before going to a store, make a list of items you want/need using store insert(s) as a guide to what's on sale, and match up coupons with items that you want. You save the most when items you have a coupon for are on sale also. Note that if you feel like you're "going in circles" while doing this, it's important to remember to **buy only what you need,** regardless of how low the price is!

In case you don't know, many grocery stores give double credit for most coupons, within certain restrictions.

These techniques might seem complicated, but often when a person tries one for a few weeks, it becomes easy.

53. This one is for the extremely frugal person! Consider using coffee grounds twice, as they still hold some flavor even after being used once. Just add some additional ground coffee to what you have already used. You may have to experiment a little before you'll know how much additional coffee to use, but it should be less than usual. Although re-using coffee grounds is an extreme example, the general concept is a real money-saver: use the same item several times.

54. Buy oatmeal instead of prepared cereals, or as an occasional alternative to them. Oatmeal requires just a few minutes to cook and costs a lot less. This is an example of how you can save when you avoid prepared foods. Note too that, in general, instant oatmeal costs more than the kind that must be boiled.

55. Share expenses whenever this is practical. As an example, national and state parks often charge a flat fee *per vehicle* that can be split among several passengers.

56. When produce begins to show the first signs of spoiling, you might want to trim out any soft spots. Often, most of the food is still quite edible, especially if you cook it. Better yet, try to **eat, cook or freeze** produce before it starts to go bad. Use judgment of course. For example, the texture of bananas changes dramatically when they're frozen and thawed, so freezing them is not recommended unless you know it works with a specific recipe.

57. Whenever practical, <u>deal with merchants you already trust</u>. Before shopping for any major purchase, don't hesitate to ask family and friends if they know of good stores and/or trustworthy salespeople.

58. Often, you can purchase foods in large, economical containers. If you feel self-conscious about serving a condiment (e.g., ketchup) out of a very large container, buy it in bulk and pour it into smaller container(s) before offering it to guests.

59. Note that some vegetables (onions for example) are best stored in a way that prevents moisture from collecting on them, such as placing them in a hanging basket. This way, they're exposed to more air, and moisture is less likely to collect on them and cause them to spoil quickly.

60. <u>Prepare rice as a side dish</u> – it's almost always cheaper to prepare simple side dishes rather than pre-packaged ones. Add flavorings for variety. (Also, noodles can be used instead of rice.) Any spice that you like will do. Possibilities include oregano, garlic, pepper, and curry. And for the adventurous, there's hot sauce, cayenne pepper, etc. Also, bouillon, tomato sauce, butter/margarine, lemon juice, minced onion and other flavorings may be used. Be creative!

61. You might want to make your own cakes and other baked goods at home, if you don't already. Some people even think of baking as a recreational, educational *and nearly free* activity to share with their children.

62. When making meatloaf, casseroles and the like, add extra vegetables and less meat. Vegetables are almost always less expensive than meat. If you're concerned about protein, you might want to add to your diet eggs, dairy products, tuna and/or peanuts.

63. Don't put bananas in the refrigerator. This makes them spoil faster. (They *can* be frozen for later use in certain recipes.)

64. If you buy carbonated beverages, consider two-liter or three-liter bottles. They're almost always cheaper (per fluid ounce) than smaller bottles or cans, partly because you end up paying for the drink, and not for a lot of containers. Note that the unit price of these drinks can be three or four times as high when purchased in single-serving cans or bottles than when purchased in two-liter or three-liter bottles. **This principle (of buying a product in larger containers to get a better unit price) holds true for almost all products.**

65. <u>Delay purchases when it is practical to do so</u>. When you think you have found the lowest price on a "big ticket item", you might want to wait for a few weeks or longer. Holiday sales or other special event sales may come along, or you might find out about a better deal from a friend or neighbor. **Also, delaying a purchase means that you might earn interest on the money you would have spent!**

66. <u>Eat at home</u> as much as is practical, considering your lifestyle. We pay a very high "premium" for eating in restaurants. Consider eating an <u>occasional</u> meal at an upscale restaurant. This is in contrast to <u>regularly</u> eating at restaurants where, perhaps without realizing it, you can spend a lot of money per week or per month.

67. <u>Make your own lunch</u> to take with you to work or school. Especially if you're "pressed for time," you might want to take items you've chilled or frozen ahead of time. They'll stay cool for quite a while, and won't spoil quickly except in extreme heat. Some people save time by preparing and freezing several lunches at one time.

68. Another option for saving money has to do with foods that are good when heated in a microwave oven. You can put lunch-sized portions of foods like soup, casseroles, meatloaf, and noodle or rice dishes into small microwave-safe containers. Freeze or refrigerate them as appropriate and take one with you to work/school each day. To save the most money, do this every day or nearly every day as this will allow you to reduce considerably the total that you spend in restaurants. (If you're a homemaker and/or you run a business at home, you can still use these techniques to reduce your spending in restaurants and to help others in your household to do the same.)

69. Consider whether you can reduce your use of meat products, which are expensive compared to many other foods. Getting enough protein is important, but protein can be found in many other kinds of foods, such as nuts, beans and dairy products. Reducing your meat consumption might sound like giving up something you love, but you don't need to give up meat entirely to save money. You might find pleasure in the great variety of available fruits, breads, vegetables, spices, etc. **Note that some people have food allergies or other concerns that should be considered before making**

dietary changes.

70. <u>Try to anticipate all holidays and other special occasions</u> and act early to save the most money. For example, around the Fourth of July, hot dogs often are discounted, but ketchup and mustard might not routinely be discounted in your area. So, buy ketchup and mustard well in advance and while it is being discounted. (It is assumed in this example that at least one person in your household *will use* these condiments.) With non-perishable items like gift wrap, your best deals are almost always available <u>after</u> holidays.

71. If you like to spend time in the kitchen, consider making your own mayonnaise, bread, cakes, etc. These recipes are relatively simple and can be found in cookbooks, of course, in many local libraries, and on the internet.

72. When preparing foods that lose little if any quality when frozen, cook larger quantities than the amount you (and others in your home) plan to eat immediately. Then freeze portions to be eaten later. The plastic bags that bread is sold in make excellent (and essentially free) containers for many items. Be aware though, that these bread bags are not completely airtight, so double-wrapping them using two bags is often advisable.

73. <u>Buy simple things</u>. Example: buy a simple desk lamp instead of paying for the installation of custom lighting. Even if it doesn't cost very much, an item like a lamp can be attractive or even elegant. Other examples include purchasing simple household products, and buying simple clothing instead of the fanciest clothing items.

74. Go to stores only when you really need to go. Simplistic? Well, maybe. But nearly all of us have gone to the same shopping center twice or more in a single day, due to changing circumstances and/or poor planning. Making fewer trips can help you save on vehicle expenses and likely will reduce your overall buying.

75. If you drink beer, you might consider buying a less expensive brand. All beers are made with the same main ingredient: water, and the other ingredients differ little from beer to beer. Many of the remaining price differences are due to: the beer's market "image"; the amount spent on marketing and advertising; the distance a beer is shipped; the cost of containers; and the volume in which it is produced. Shop around some until you find a beer you like that also has reasonable price.

76. <u>Buy fresh fruits and vegetables in bulk when their prices are low</u> and consider freezing or canning them. But be sure not to buy so much that they'll spoil before you can eat, can or freeze them. If you can them, follow canning instructions carefully to make sure the food will remain safe to eat.

77. Buy from the bulk food sections that some food stores offer, in which products are stored in large containers like barrels or bins and then placed by the customer into plastic bags. But shop carefully – sometimes, traditionally packaged items are still cheaper when they're on sale.

78. Avoid buying items in fancy packaging or those that are over-packaged. Certain snack foods are good examples. Some are sold in a box, and inside of the box is a bag. When people buy items like these, they pay for a lot of packaging they will throw away immediately.

79. Buy soy sauce when it's on sale. It can be used to add a tremendous amount of flavor to many types of dishes including fish and chicken entrees. **(Note that some people may have health-related concerns here as some soy sauce varieties are high in sodium and/or contain some alcohol.)**

80. After each meal, be sure to save your "leftovers". Look for creative ways to use the leftovers to create additional main dishes. For these additional dishes, casseroles are a good choice, because potatoes or meat, for example, can be added to other ingredients, creating a dish that can sometimes seem like a completely different meal.

81. Consider the use of spices in foods that you cook. If you use them already, use them more creatively to turn simple foods like potatoes, rice and pasta into wonderful meals at reasonable prices. Many spices add a great deal of flavor to food given their cost. Although some spices are expensive, some are not as expensive as they seem when used wisely, and some aren't expensive at all.

In almost all cases, you can buy spices in a "raw" form for a small fraction of the cost of powdered spices that are sold in tiny bottles. Examples of spices in raw form are garlic, hot peppers and ginger, each of which can be found in the produce section of many supermarkets.

82. You might want to buy and use cabbage in recipes. In many places, cabbage is one of the least expensive foods available, and it can be served in a variety of ways, including salads, sauerkraut, and cole slaw.

83. This tip is for those who eat a substantial amount of meat. It's probably worth checking with the manager of the meat department at the grocery store you visit most to ask which day of the week they usually offer their best discounts. (Supermarkets often base some of their discounting decisions on the delivery schedules for products they carry.)

84. For at least some of your meals each week, plan the meals based on what your local grocery store(s) are selling that week at a discounted price. Also take into account what food items you have on hand already that should be used soon.

85. <u>Before you buy a new item, take a little time to consider buying a used one instead</u>. It's important to consider, for almost any item, its condition and sometimes the way it has been handled or maintained. However, if a used product meets your wants/needs, you can often save a large amount of money compared to the purchase of a new product. To help make this a habit, you might want to remember the phrase, **"Think used first."** For some kinds of used items like used books, clothes and video games, there are even individual stores dedicated to the re-sale of just one particular type of product.

86. Consider a return to buying simple products that have been available for fifty years or more. These would including many familiar products like vanilla wafers, popcorn, ginger snaps, aspirin, gelatin, etc. The best deals are most often obtained when buying these items in the simplest available packaging. If you already buy some of these, you might consider buying others, too.

Household Items and Services

87. Don't throw away pants that have been "outgrown" or have gone out of style before you consider making a pair of shorts out of them or handing them down to a younger family member. Making shorts out of a pair of pants is, of course, an example of converting an item to meet a different need rather than discarding the item.

88. Don't buy things you won't use. This may sound too simple to even mention, but in truth, sometimes a few extra moments of thought and perhaps self-control can help people to avoid making unnecessary purchases. Try to be sure that an item is something you will actually use when you get it home.

89. Be creative in re-using things. Below are a few possibilities that won't be right for everyone, but that could provide insight into new ways of re-using common items.

An old metal wastebasket, if it's still sturdy, can be repainted, then turned upside-down to make a little stand for use either outdoors or in a place like a utility room.

A dinner plate that has a small imperfection, or which doesn't match your other plates, could be used as the base for a small planter.

Wooden boards that were once parts of an old fence, with proper attention to safety, can become a set of shelves for use in a shed or garage.

Many people throw away old tires. In some locations though, it is permissible to use an old tire as part of a rope swing.

If you "recycle" a tire by using it in a new way, you have, in effect, created a "new" item at no cost. (In some cases, you will have also avoided a disposal fee.) In the same way, many other items can be used in creative ways that might not be obvious.

A decorative bowl that has become chipped or that has lost its shine might still be used outdoors as a planter or as an ash tray. A little bit of leftover gravel or pebbles from a landscaping project can be used in the bottom of planters to provide better drainage for plants.

It's likely that almost everyone has heard of clothing that ends up being used by more than one child; many people call these items "hand-me-downs." Whenever this isn't a practical option, old clothes can always be kept for use in the most obvious way: as rags.

A bookcase that no longer fits the decor in your living room, or that simply has become old or unattractive, might still be used in an attic or basement.

90. <u>Consider replacing part of an item rather that the entire item, whenever appropriate.</u> One example, in which the difference in costs is rather large, is replacing the tiny washer inside a faucet to stop it from dripping, rather than replacing the entire faucet.

91. Remember that friends or family members sometimes have the background knowledge and/or specialized equipment to clean or repair items instead of your having to pay "professional rates" to have these services done. If you don't know someone who can do repairs for you at a reduced cost (or free), your friends/family often can recommend companies and workers with whom they have had good experiences. If you use companies that you "find" in, for example, the phone book, be sure to get written estimates and compare several possible service providers.

92. If you pay a company to do lawn or yard work,

consider instead paying neighborhood kids to do some or all of the work. They often work for less money, and the experience tends to teach children about work and earning money. Naturally, you'll want to be sure they have parental permission and that their work environment will be safe.

93. <u>Do things yourself</u>. This idea may seem simplistic, but often, people pay to have a job done even though they have the time and skills to do the job themselves.

94. Consider buying items at thrift shops instead of buying new things. In many places, charities run stores selling used items that often have been cleaned and refurbished for resale. Tremendous savings are possible in stores like these, although finding appropriate sizes and styles can be a problem, especially for items like clothing and jewelry.

95. You might want to learn to sew on buttons and do other tasks involved in mending clothes, if you don't know how already. Potentially, this single action can save you a lot of money over time, as it can extend, often by several years, the useful "life" of an article of clothing.

96. Buy re-useable filters, if available, then wash them as needed, instead of buying new filters. This can apply to your furnace filter, portable air cleaners, etc.

97. Before buying any "big-ticket" item, consider who will be using it and try to share the cost. For example, if you have roommates and need a new lawn mower, you might ask the roommates to share the cost with you. (There's even a small chance one of them might help mow the lawn!)

98. Lemon juice can be used to add a lot of flavor to

food and drinks for very little money. If you drink a lot of cola, you might want to try adding about one teaspoon of lemon juice and some water to each cup, creating a soft drink that tastes good but that costs much less per serving. (When you pour the soft drink into a glass, fill the glass only to about three-fourths full. Then add the lemon juice and water. Experiment with these quantities to suit your own taste. Some people will want to add a little sugar; others can actually enjoy the natural sour taste of lemon without any extra sugar.) You can choose to do this only sometimes, or not at all, of course. If you use the method described above, you could save about as much as if you paid 25% less for the product.

99. Try to use *simple* cleaning products. (Here, the word "simple" refers to simple ingredients and simple packaging.) Fancy packaging and glitzy advertising might draw attention to a product, but they are not necessarily associated with products that actually work better. However, heavily advertised products almost always cost more than store brands. **Try not to pay extra for heavily- advertised products.**

As an example of simpler cleaning products, plain window cleaner can be purchased in large economical sizes, and it works on counter tops, most plastics, glass items, etc. (It's not recommended for items made of wood.) Baking soda in water cleans and deodorizes refrigerators and other appliances. Note that baking soda is a mild abrasive -- it has been known to leave scratch marks, so use great care if using baking soda on very fine items like silver or fine china.

Vinegar is excellent for removing soap scum, and for cleaning coffee makers, tea kettles, etc. (Note: If you use vinegar to clean a coffee maker, follow the manufacturer's recommendations.)

100. <u>Make your own</u> simple products. One example is window cleaner, which you can make using one part white vinegar and six parts water.

101. <u>Make use of local sales such as yard sales</u> or those provided by churches, scouting troops and the like. But be sure not to buy things you don't need.

102. Remember to take a few minutes to <u>be sure clothing fits well before buying it</u>.

103. Those who use a conditioner (also called "creme rinse" by some people) after shampooing can save money when they begin using a very tiny amount of conditioner. The key is to leave the conditioner in your hair rather than rinsing it out. For most people, a bead of conditioner that's about the size of a pearl will work fine.

104. Instead of throwing away sponges that have

become heavily soiled, sanitize them with very hot water -- some people put them it in the top rack of their dishwasher. This is an example of how you can save money when you <u>clean an item rather than throwing it out</u>. **But use a twist tie to secure the sponges so they can't fall and block the drain inside your dishwasher.**

105. You might want to try using less of personal care products like toothpaste and shampoo. Many ads for these products subtly suggest how much to use. For example, a professional model is shown (on TV or in print) using shampoo. It's in the company's best interests for customers to use as much shampoo as possible, so the model is seen using a handful of shampoo, although normally much less is needed. <u>Consider, as a test, using one-third less of personal care products</u> -- you'll likely experience no difference in the results. (Note that when shampooing, you only need enough shampoo to break up the oil in your hair.)

106. When you have just a bit of liquid detergent left in a bottle, add some water to it, put the cap back on the bottle, and shake the bottle vigorously. Upon removing the cap, you'll find a surprising amount of useable suds. This technique can of course be used with many kinds of products including window cleaner, hand soap, laundry soap, shampoo and dishwasher soap. Be very careful not to spill anything while diluting products, as that would reduce or eliminate any savings.

107. <u>Consider making your own</u> holiday and/or birthday cards. This almost always saves money compared with buying cards. Also, making cards yourself (or as a family) shows a personal touch. Some people just aren't very good at this kind of craft. If you're not sure, you could spend a half an hour or so trying it. If the cards don't look as nice as you want them to, you can abandon the idea and buy some cards. You won't have lost much. If you *can* make attractive cards, you could save a fair amount of money several times per year and indefinitely.

108. Make arts and crafts yourself rather that paying for them. A little fabric or some nic-nacs (plus some imagination and maybe a bit of paint) can add accents and color to a room for a fraction of the cost of store-bought items. There are now more specialty stores than ever which sell a huge variety of materials for arts and crafts projects.

109. Consider using simple, inexpensive baking soda as a supplement to toothpaste or as a mildly abrasive cleanser.

110. Soap, pine cones, cinnamon sticks or other aromatic items can be placed in a decorative basket to add a fresh scent to the air in a room. This can reduce or eliminate purchases of more expensive air fresheners.

111. Try to select clothing that lasts a long time and is unlikely to go out of style. Blue jeans are a good example.

112. <u>Try to remain open-minded</u> about different styles/sizes of products. For example, if you are used to a full-length bathrobe and need to replace it, you might find that you can buy a somewhat shorter bathrobe for much less. Each of us has certain tastes, of course, but you might find that you can adapt in ways that will save you a lot of money over the years. As another example, you might like the aroma of a particular household cleaner, but over perhaps a few weeks, you might get accustomed to a less fragrant store brand that costs much less.

113. <u>Reduce your use of store-bought cleaning</u>

products. With some exceptions like fine furniture, you can dust many items with a feather duster, or clean articles with a moist cloth or sponge instead of an expensive store-bought dusting product.

114. Consider that sometimes you can <u>clean things with water</u> instead of using store-bought products. Water has been called the "universal solvent," meaning that it will dissolve many substances. Note that water will not dissolve fat, oil or grease, but that simple soaps and detergents will.

115. You might want to get haircuts done (for you or your family) by a friend, relative or neighbor. Many people who are not considered professionals are quite competent at cutting hair.

116. Buy holiday cards, birthday cards, etc. in sets rather than one at a time, or make your own cards!

117. Avoid buying small items (note pads, sponges, etc.) one at a time. It's usually a better value to <u>buy several</u> in a pre-packaged assortment.

118. <u>Look for close-outs</u> on clothing and other items. (For those who don't know, these are items that retailers are planning to remove from the items that they carry.) A true close-out is a rare case in which a retailer is a "motivated seller."

119. If you use a lot of batteries, you might want to use rechargeable batteries, or use an AC adapter if available for the item in question. Either of these options likely will pay for itself over time as you buy fewer batteries.

120. If you are not especially sensitive to the "feel" of fabrics, you might not need to buy fabric softener, especially if you use a detergent that contains a pleasant smell. In addition, some people are sensitive to fabrics that feel dry or scratchy, but this is much more noticeable in winter (when humidity is often low) than at other times of the year. As a result, some people find that they like to buy fabric softener mostly for the winter months, but that they can do without it for much of the rest of the year.

121. <u>Store brands are almost always a better value</u> than brand name products. A likely exception is when a "name brand" item is on sale *and* you have a manufacturer's coupon.

122. If you have children, use the "hand-me-down" method for more than just clothing. Games, bicycles and other personal belongings can be handed down, especially if the older child receives (or has already received) an item that meets his or her wants or needs.

123. It's so simple, but we all sometimes still fail to do it: <u>hang on to what you have</u>. Take simple steps to keep from losing things. Put your name and phone number inside items of children's clothing, and consider writing this information in or on personal items like books, cell phones, suitcases, etc.

124. Avoid buying disposable cups. Use the cups you already have in your kitchen.

125. If you have a dishwasher, don't run it until it's full or very close to full. Running it sooner is a waste of electricity, water, detergent and your time.

126. Except possibly for special occasions, avoid buying plastic knives, forks and spoons. Simply use your own flatware. Note that yard sales are a great place to find bargains on kitchen items.

127. Avoid buying paper towels. You might want to hang a cloth towel on the handle of your refrigerator (or in a similar spot) and use it to clean up small messes. Then sanitize it as needed. If you buy paper towels, you can still save money if you remember that for the littlest messes such as small spills, you can often use just a part of a sheet instead of a whole paper towel.

128. Avoid plates, cups, etc. that are made of glass or porcelain. They break. Instead, consider buying and using items that are made of plastic or another durable material.

129. If you have outdated letterhead or other stationery, you might want to turn it over and use it as scratch paper, or when practical, as fax paper or paper to be used in a computer printer.

130. If you have business cards printed, it's usually best to have no more the 500 to 1,000 printed. Even though the per-card price is usually much better when purchasing higher quantities, this is only important if you will use the cards! **Don't buy what you don't need.** For most people, five hundred or a thousand cards will last for several years, and in the meantime, some piece of information (address, job title, etc.) is very likely to change. So, don't order too many cards, even though some printers might try to sell you thousands of them.

131. If you have outdated business cards, you can still use the backs of them for phone messages, grocery lists, etc.

132. Consider buying desk and office supplies in bulk at a discount office supply store. For example, you can buy a three-year supply of tape at a good price instead of buying it one roll at a time at a grocery or drug store.

133. Re-use some or all of the bags that you receive at the grocery store. They can be used for storing items, lining waste baskets, disposing of yard waste or cat litter, etc. If you don't re-use them, you might want to consider recycling them at your grocery store (if available) or through any community recycling program. Many items besides bags are, of course, recyclable.

134. Consider making some of your purchases in consignment shops. They sometimes have high-quality clothing, etc., at very low prices. Pay special attention to their terms of sale, as at some stores, items might not be returnable even if they are defective. However, if you check items carefully before you buy, this should rarely be a problem, and you might find some excellent bargains.

135. Consider anything that you collect on a regular basis, such as coins, movies, music, etc. Most people have several kinds of collections to give some thought to. Then, think about whether you spend reasonably on the items, or if you may have, over time, increased your purchases to a level that isn't justifiable. Key points to consider are whether you still take time to enjoy most of what you've already collected, and whether you have gradually begun to spend money in a compulsive or habitual manner.

136. Some people are talented enough as artists to make gifts for people rather than buying them. You could begin doing some simple arts and crafts at home to see what abilities you have; then decide which creations are good enough to be used as gifts. Another option is to make everyday items with a "home-made touch," such as scented soaps or candles, or food items such as fresh bread, brownies, pies, etc.

137. <u>Search for coupons on the internet</u> for items that you know you will be purchasing. For example, if you'll be buying pet food, you can search for the terms: "pet food" and "coupon" – and specifying a brand name if you (or your pet) have a preference. (Remember, if you don't have internet access at home, many libraries offer free access, including the ability to print items.)

138. With some kinds of water-based products such as shampoo, conditioner, liquid soap (including dishwasher soap) and moisturizer, it's possible save money by watering them down. Just assemble all of the appropriate items in one place. Then, for each container, look at the amount of liquid in it and add about about one-fourth of that amount of water to it. Remember that afterward, the products will flow more quickly from the containers, so squeeze them gently. <u>Don't try this with items for which water can cause a problem. Examples include lubricating oil and similar products that are used with vehicles and other machinery; adding water to these can lead to serious problems with rust</u>.

139. Look for websites that list and/or compare

opportunities for saving money. Those with internet access can search for keywords like "money-saving" or "cheap".

Here are a few examples of these kinds of sites:

StreetPrices.com

DailyeDeals.com

PriceGrabber.com

CurrentCodes.com

RetailMeNot.com

Shopping-Bargains.com

KeepCash.com

DotDeals.com

140. <u>Try using simple cocoa butter as a moisturizer</u>. A small container can last for months and often costs much less than other moisturizers.

Housing Costs

141. If you remodel your home, consider having your refrigerator placed away from both your stove, and from any other considerable source of heat such as direct sunlight. This change will make the refrigerator's "job" easier. Although it would represent a small potential savings, it's one that could have an effect for decades. For example, if this move saved only five cents per day, the total savings over thirty years would be more than $500.00.

142. Periodically consider moving to a different location where your total costs (including housing costs, transportation, living expenses, etc.) will be lower. You might want to put a reminder on your calendar, so that you'll reconsider this question, for example, once each year.

143. Try always to be prepared for "normal" bills such as housing costs and utilities. If you can afford to, keep money set aside for them. This will help you to avoid late fees and similar fees/penalties. If you can't afford to do this, it's very likely that your normal bills are higher than they should be.

144. If it fits your lifestyle, get one or more roommates/housemates who can pay rent to you and share expenses. This can be a huge financial benefit regardless of whether you are a renter or homeowner. Roommates also can share information about bargains, sale items and coupons. Just be sure to check out any potential renter's background and/or reputation before renting to them. Also, note that if *you* are a renter, there might be restrictions on you renting out any portion of the premises, so check the terms of your lease.

145. Consider refinancing your home when interest

rates are _approximately_ two percent (2%) less than your current loan. However, this guideline applies only if you'll keep your present home long enough that your savings will exceed any out-of-pocket charges. **Other exceptions and considerations, including tax considerations, exist and vary from person to person. It is often wise to consult trusted adviser(s) and/or do research before refinancing or borrowing money in any other way.**

146. If you decide to refinance, consider consulting a mortgage broker. They often have experience with the selection of options such as: interest rate and "points" combinations, lenders, and appraisers. Also, they should be, and often are, _independent_ of other organizations in the real estate industry. Although there is no guarantee of independence, you can be sure that a loan officer (for example) is _not_ independent of the bank he or she works for. Many loan officers are undoubtedly good and helpful people, but it's part of their job to get a good deal *for the bank*, even if this means *you* don't get a very good deal. <u>Unless you're already an expert, it's often wise to do some research before refinancing in order to learn more about the process and your options</u>. **Also, consult people you already know and trust.**

Information and Entertainment

147. If you have a computer, consider buying information and entertainment (books, games, music, etc.) on CD-ROMs instead of the "old-fashioned" forms. You will often save money on the item, it's usually possible to make a backup copy in case you lose your original, and you'll save space in your home.

148. You might live in a city or town that has at least one store which will pay for used books. The payments are often small, but receiving any amount is better than getting nothing at all. If you ever have books that you want to get rid of, go ahead and get paid for turning in what you might have disposed of in some other way.

149. Treat "junk mail" sales pitches with skepticism, or even suspicion. With few exceptions, companies sending you this mail are spending a lot on postage, envelopes, marketing research, etc. They pass these costs on to you. If you don't do it already, you might want to routinely throw junk mail into the trash. Then, instead of responding to junk mail pitches, you could do the following: when you need or want specific products or services, actively seek out and compare companies that offer those products or services.

You can use recommendations from friends/relatives and do your own searching using the internet, phone books and/or other directories. In short, you should <u>seek out what you need, instead of letting sellers tell you what they think you need</u>.

150. When possible, don't buy reading material. Instead, use the internet and/or any free library in your area.

151. <u>Periodically examine bills that relate to information</u>

or entertainment for ways that you might save money. For example, if you subscribe to cable (or satellite) TV and there are channels you don't watch, see if you can switch to a "channel package" that costs less because it provides fewer channels – but ones that you will actually watch. Also, you might want to consider free or less expensive activities (sports, hobbies, exercise, reading, social groups, music, board games, crafts, investment clubs, travel, etc.) **Often, gradually switching to new activities can save a lot of money with little or no "pain."**

Cable television can be great for entertainment and certain kinds of information, but there are a lot of other options, and many of them are free. Another way to save is to be sure you own as much of the equipment as possible rather than renting it. This only applies, of course, if you'll keep the service (or a compatible one) long enough to recoup what you paid for the equipment.

152. If you plan to send a child (or anyone) to college or to a private school, consider taking advantage of any scholarships or reduced-cost loans that are offered by governments, private foundations and/or the colleges themselves. You can begin your research on these options online and/or at your local library. Give yourself plenty of time for research before the anticipated time of enrollment. In addition, for those who prefer computer software for doing research, software packages are available which are designed to assist in the selection and comparison of colleges and universities.

Start a college fund as soon as possible after a child is born. It's surprising how much an investment can grow over eighteen years. Also, some states have programs that give parents or guardians a special deal if they pay for (or begin paying for) a child's education years in advance. Sometimes, parents can "lock in" the cost of a college education at today's prices and pay for it over several years, and some educational expenses are tax deductible. You might want to contact your state department of education for more information, or check into it at a local library. Remember: librarians can be very helpful, especially during hours when the library is less crowded.

153. If you plan to send a child to college, bear in mind that <u>tuition is often lower at colleges in your own state</u>.

154. If you subscribe to newspapers or magazines, consider which one(s) you read the most. If they don't give you much "bang for the buck," don't renew them. In some cases, if you cancel a subscription, you can even get a partial refund, but sometimes that only happens if you ask for the refund.

155. Look for simple types of recreation and entertainment. For example, many communities have free outdoor amusements such as tennis courts, soccer fields, hiking trails, etc. Also, many local libraries offer computers for short-term use while in the library, and some offer free access to the internet.

156. If you are an avid reader, you might want to build friendships with other people who like to read, and lend books to each other. This can help you buy fewer books while getting to read more of them.

157. Some kinds of entertainment and recreation (such as movies, parks and miniature golf) offer a booklet of tickets that will save you money over time. Be sure that if the tickets have expiration date(s), you'll use them before the tickets expire.

158. If you play computer-based games and/or video

games, consider a key issue when buying another one: How many times are you likely to play the game? There is a big difference between paying a considerable amount (let's use fifty dollars as an example) for a game you'll use 500 times over the course of many years, and paying the same amount for a game you will play only ten times before becoming bored with it. It's often important that a game has several game variations or themes instead of just a single way to play the game. When possible, try out any game thoroughly before buying it.

Travel and Vacations

159. Nearly everyone should buy the cheapest gasoline available. The extra money some people pay for gasoline pays for things such as advertising, higher profit margins for retailers, and "secret additives" of dubious value. (Nearly all cars will run quite well on regular gasoline. Note that *some* older cars may require a higher-octane gasoline to run properly.)

160. If you take the bus on a regular basis, compare the cost of a weekly "bus pass" (or similar options that might be available) to the cost of paying a separate fare each time you ride. Also, many subway systems have similar programs.

161. <u>Save on fuel</u> by driving at fifty miles per hour or slower, **but only when it's safe to do so**. In fact, the most fuel-efficient speed for many cars is between forty-five and fifty-five miles per hour.

162. Use great care to <u>drive safely</u>. It can, in addition to saving lives, save you a tremendous amount of money over the years by keeping to a minimum your expenses for car insurance, car repairs, medical bills, etc. Remember that a single serious accident can leave people unable to earn a living, cost thousands of dollars now, *and* make you pay more in insurance premiums for many years to come. At the risk of sounding "preachy," this topic is so important, <u>that this it's worth saying one more time: Drive Safely</u>! For anyone who's interested, some of the most important things to remember about safe driving are:

(1) <u>Don't be overconfident</u> -- many of us tend to *feel* very powerful behind the wheel, but the truth is we're vulnerable. (2) <u>Watch out for "other drivers"</u> -- people make mistakes every day, and some drivers are just plain

reckless. (3) <u>Maintain a reasonable speed</u> -- being in a hurry simply doesn't justify irresponsible driving that can cause deaths and serious injuries. (4) <u>Don't Tailgate</u> - tailgating makes it difficult or impossible to react to trouble in front of you, and in some cases makes it impossible to even *see* trouble emerging ahead. (5) <u>Don't drive while you're under the influence of any drug</u> that impairs your driving skills. This includes alcohol and certain prescriptions, and the rule applies regardless of whether it's a legal or an illegal drug, and regardless of how well you believe you're able to drive. (6) <u>Stay Alert</u> -- and this includes being aware of what is happening <u>some distance ahead</u> of your vehicle, *and* what is happening behind you (check your rear view mirrors often). (7) <u>Consider the weather and lighting conditions</u> when you drive... and use your headlights and other lights <u>whenever they might help other drivers to see you</u>... and the headlights, of course, will help *you* to see, also. **(8)**

Wear your seat belts, and insist that everyone in the vehicle does the same! Finally, note that there is another side to some of these rules. For example, while overconfidence can be very dangerous, it's important to develop a reasonable level of confidence -- a belief that as long as you pay attention and do the right things, you'll almost always be just fine.

163. When vacationing, consider campgrounds or cabins instead of motels and hotels.

164. Find someone to travel with you when you go shopping and when you travel for leisure. Share expenses with them. Examples: gasoline, meals, maps, groceries, motels/lodging. Often, two or more people can travel with less expense (per person) than one person traveling alone.

165. When you'll be away from home for a few days or

weeks, be sure to ask a neighbor you can trust to watch your house for you and give it a "lived-in look." The expenses associated with thefts and break-ins can be enormous. Police in some communities will (if asked) be especially vigilant while you're away, driving past your home occasionally, as time permits.

166. For those who want to visit national parks in the United States, the National Park Service (**http://www.nps.gov**) offers savings through the "America the Beautiful" program, which allows many visits for a flat fee during a single one-year period. For seniors, the cost is much lower.

167. When traveling, bring along food to reduce money spent at restaurants. Be sure to choose foods that don't spoil easily. When packing food items into a container, remember that you can put frozen foods on top of other foods so the latter will stay cold longer. Add ice as needed.

168. Take homemade drinks with you when traveling instead of buying them "on the road." A little planning can save several dollars per day for many people. If you buy soft drinks while traveling, consider buying them in packs of twelve or more.

169. When traveling, plan to visit free sites. Many state and federal parks, for example, are either free or require a small fee compared to the cost of commercial attractions.

170. If you don't use public transportation for at least some of your travel, consider doing so. Especially in those cities where bus/subway fares are relatively low, you can save money by reducing all of the many expenses involved in using a personal vehicle.

171. Before leaving town for a vacation or any type of recreation, remember to take any items that are specific to the type of trip you're taking. For example, if you're going to the beach, remember your sunglasses, bathing suits and sunscreen. For wintertime trips, be sure to take all of the cold weather items you might want such as thick socks, gloves, boots, etc. All of these items cost a lot more if you buy them after you arrive at a vacation spot instead of going to a discount store near your home.

172. <u>Combine several trips</u> into one. A good technique is to set aside one day per week in which to do the majority of your errands. Then decide on a route from one location to the next that will use the smallest amount of gas and put the fewest miles on your car.

Utilities

173. <u>Use the lowest wattage light bulbs that you can for the room or space where you want light</u>. For example, you might want a 100-watt bulb in your living room, but only a 60-watt bulb in a hallway. Also, compact fluorescent light bulbs offer an excellent value. In fact, for household use in the U.S., and as long as you purchase bulbs at the best prices available, it's almost always true that compact fluorescent bulbs are the best overall value, followed by traditional fluorescent bulbs. Incandescent bulbs, although more traditional in their appearance, cost more in the long run than either of the fluorescent bulb types. Note that although you'll pay more initially for a compact fluorescent bulb, they're designed to not only use less energy, but to last for a very long time.

The following table shows the dramatic reduction in

electricity usage (in watts) when switching from incandescent (sometimes called "standard") bulbs to compact fluorescent ones.

Light Bulb Comparison
Approximate Equivalents
for Watts Used

Standard		Compact Fluorescent
40 watts	=	10 watts
60 watts	=	14 watts
75 watts	=	20 watts
100 watts	=	27 watts

174. In the summertime, use a microwave oven instead of a traditional oven as much as possible, because the microwave won't heat your house to any noticeable degree. (Extra heat in the house works against your air conditioner, of course.) <u>Try to never have one appliance "fighting" with another</u>.

175. If and when possible, don't use air conditioning. It is costly and has a temporary effect -- after all, you're paying to fight Mother Nature.

176. Consider closing heating and cooling vents to any room that is not used, or is used only rarely. This may include bathrooms, attics, spare rooms, and in some cases, basements. But don't overdo it... closing off too many vents could put a strain on your home's heating/cooling system. It's usually possible to use a nearly closed position that reduces airflow without completely preventing it.

177. When using your oven in warmer months, consider turning off your air conditioner. You could also use these occasions to air out the house. As mentioned in other parts of this guidebook, try to never have two appliances "fighting with" (working against) each other.

Also, note that you might want to have a fan running while you do this, especially if the weather is humid or very warm. (Air conditioners use a tremendous amount of electricity compared to most other appliances.) **Be sure not to use this idea if anyone in your home has health concerns related to heat.**

178. Avoid indoor halogen bulbs unless you really need a great deal of light in a certain area. While they produce a lot of light, replacement bulbs are expensive compared to "standard" (incandescent) or fluorescent bulbs. (Note that some photographers and others *prefer* halogen bulbs because of the "true color rendering" quality of the light they produce.)

179. <u>Fluorescent light bulbs are almost always an excellent value.</u> The bulbs often last for several years, and they produce more light per watt of electricity used. Also, when you plan to purchase any light fixture, be sure that reasonably priced bulbs are available for it. Avoid any "specialty" or non-standard fixture unless it is the only one that meets your needs.

180. You might want to <u>lower the temperature setting on your water heater</u> so the water is just hot enough for sanitizing dishes, washing clothes, etc., and for showers. A hotter setting is a hazard and is likely a waste of money. (You might want to try changing this temperature setting very slightly at first. Reducing this temperature decreases the amount of available warm water for showers, etc., so if two or more people take showers before your water heater has a chance to "catch up", someone could get a cold shower!) This technique works best in households with only one or two people, where hot water usage is relatively more predictable. Also, put insulation around your water heater (and hot water pipes), but **for gas-fired units, be careful not to block the flow of air to the area around the pilot light.**

181. You can save quite a bit if you <u>wash clothing in warm or even cold water</u>, at least for many loads. (First, check the label on your detergent to be sure that it works at these temperatures.) Also, depending on what you're washing, you might need a bit of bleach and/or a longer wash cycle to be sure clothes truly become clean.

182. <u>If you own your own home, be sure it is well insulated</u>. If you rent, you might want to ask the property owner to pay for insulation or share the expense with you. In either case, consider how long you plan to stay in your current home before investing a lot in insulation. Note: insulation is assigned an "R rating" that indicates how well it insulates.

183. If you pay per-minute rates for phone usage, <u>share expenses</u> on phone calls to relatives. This can be especially helpful at holiday gatherings when many calls are often made. Remember that several people can talk during a single phone call. The most expensive minute of a call is almost always the first minute.

184. Compare your current long distance phone service with other services that might meet your needs, if you haven't done so recently. There are more options available than ever. **Note: some local phone service providers charge a fee when you switch to a different long-distance provider.** However, some long-distance companies will give you a credit for this amount when you switch to their service.

185. Consider whether "caller ID" is a better deal compared with pay-per-use callback service. (Each of these services can be thought of as the telephone equivalent of a peephole that lets you see who is or was "calling.") **Most off all, consider whether you need either service or want it enough to pay any extra cost.**

186. To reduce your telephone bill, consider whether measured service or unlimited service is better for you. Consumers can save money if their local phone company offers limited service options that will eliminate your paying for a level of service you don't actually use. An example is a plan that would allow one-hundred outgoing local calls per month for a low, flat rate. Note that these options have become more and more scarce over time as the cost of phone services in general have dropped.

187. You can save money when you <u>use light bulbs that have a low wattage</u> for outdoor lighting. It's often possible to increase safety and still save money by using light bulbs with lower wattages and putting them in more locations. (For example, two 40-watt bulbs use less energy than one 100-watt bulb.) The idea is to have the right amount of light in the right places. **Safety first, however... try to keep outdoor areas effectively lit to**

avoid falls and to provide increased security.

188. <u>Turn off TVs, computers and other appliances</u> when not in use. You'll reduce wear and tear on the equipment and decrease your electric bill.

189. <u>Turn off lights that are not needed.</u> You also could encourage others in your household to do the same thing. What's simpler than flipping a switch? Still, many homes routinely have several lights in use which are not being used.

190. <u>Try not to run water unnecessarily</u>, as many people do for the entire time that they're brushing their teeth. In the kitchen, try to run water only when filling the sink or while rinsing an item, not while washing an entire set of dishes or while cleaning all of your counter tops, etc. If children or others in your household tend to let the water run while brushing teeth, etc., it's usually possible to at least reduce the rate of flow by turning the shutoff valve located under the sink.

191. A household's overall water usage is affected greatly by the amount of water used by the toilets. It may sound silly, but you might want to place a brick inside the toilet tank. **(To prevent any malfunction or damage, be sure to place the brick away from the toilet's functional parts, and don't block the flow of water.)** This often reduces water bills significantly because less water is used with each flush. Securely wrap the brick in thick plastic before placing it in the toilet tank. This should prevent any brick fragments from blocking water flow.

192. Be careful what you throw away. Many items can be sold for at least a small amount of money. But remember, **safety first: any dangerous items should**

be disposed of properly.

193. Consider the heat produced by the sun. During daylight hours, you might: in summer, close your blinds or curtains; and in winter, open them to allow warmth into the house. Think of the sun in the wintertime as free solar heating and lighting. **Once again though, remember safety and security issues should come first, and some people believe that it's safer to keep blinds/curtains closed whenever no one is home.**

194. If you have an attic, consider using a properly-installed attic fan to help remove heat from your house during warmer months.

195. When forty- or sixty-watt bulbs are on sale, almost everyone should buy them. (If you're using compact fluorescent bulbs, buy bulbs that produce an equivalent amount of light – see the table in item 6.) Lower wattage bulbs are sometimes difficult to find, but they'll save you money on your electric bill.

It's important to note that lower wattage bulbs are too dim for some purposes, especially when used alone in a given location. If you're in doubt, experiment at first by buying just a few lower-wattage bulbs and trying them in locations that seem to have enough light or more light than they need. Remember also that it's possible to increase your use of sunlight by opening curtains and blinds.

196. Be aware that even if a light fixture (lamp, vanity, ceiling fan, etc.) has sockets for several bulbs, you don't have to put a <u>working</u> bulb in every socket. **Safety first, of course: don't leave a socket empty, as doing so could allow someone could get a shock from it. Instead, leave a "burned out" bulb in the socket.**

197. <u>Examine your phone bills carefully</u>. Although billing is usually accurate, phone companies, like other organizations, do make mistakes. In the case of any charges that are clearly unwarranted, many phone companies will adjust your bill without much of a "hassle."

198. You might want to encourage your "long-distance" friends to telephone you. This is especially important for friends and acquaintances who tend to "go on and on" when talking on the phone. If they talk for a long time, then why not let them pay for the calls? It might seem callous, but it's really what's fair.

199. You might politely ask people who visit you to be courteous by <u>turning off lights and appliances</u> that aren't being used. Most people will understand because they have their own bills to pay.

200. <u>Use a fan in summer</u> instead of, or as a

supplement to, your air conditioner. **When using air conditioning, using a fan too lets you raise the thermostat about five degrees with no change in how cool the air feels.** This is, believe it or not, a "wind-chill affect" that works to your advantage. A ceiling fan works especially well – set it to pull cool air upward in summer and pull warm air downward in winter (if your ceiling fan has a switch to control the fan's direction of rotation).

201. <u>Reduce your use of indoor lights during the summer</u>. Light bulbs put out a surprising amount of heat. Using fewer lights will reduce your air conditioning costs somewhat. In summer, you also might want to shift to using fluorescent light bulbs where practical. They produce less heat than incandescent bulbs. (As mentioned earlier, they also last longer and use less energy.)

202. Some people place a small, inexpensive battery-powered light between their bedroom and a nearby bathroom so they don't have to use "house lights" for any middle-of-the-night bathroom visits. This can reduce your electric bill. Naturally, several of these lights can be used to accommodate multiple bedrooms and bathrooms.

203. If you own a home and plan to keep it for at least a year or two, be sure you have a programmable thermostat. This kind of thermostat can be set to save on energy costs by keeping your heating/cooling system turned off for several hours while no one is home – usually this is during the day while everyone is at work or at school. If your home doesn't have this type of thermostat, try to have one installed when you're already having an electrician or handyman visit your home to do other work anyway. Doing so should save on the total amount of the worker's time (and a possible "trip charge") that you will have to pay for.

204. If your and/or others in your household have cellular phones, consider getting rid of any "land line" or "hard wired" phones that you have.

Vehicles

205. If you own a car, try to <u>do tune-ups yourself</u>, or find a friend or neighbor who can do them for a reasonable fee.

206. If you're a very good driver and your car is getting old, consider dropping the collision coverage. **This is a very personal decision that depends on your driving skills and your willingness to take the financial risk of having less insurance.** But note that with insurance premiums, part of what you pay goes toward items like salaries, the insurance company's legal fees, administrative costs associated with tracking insurance claims, and to other overhead costs.

207. <u>Keep enough air in your car's tires</u>. Check your tire pressure at least once per month. Keeping them properly inflated can dramatically increase your gas mileage.

208. Consider buying a used car instead of a new one. Buying a new car means paying a premium price simply because it's new, and its value drops immediately after buying it. Buying a used car almost always means you get more for your money, **but be sure to have any used car checked by someone who's qualified to assess its condition.**

209. Look for "motivated sellers", especially on big-ticket items like cars. (A motivated seller is someone with a special reason for wanting to sell.) **Examples: the seller is unable to make their loan payments or the seller indicates that they "must" have a newer/better/faster car.**

210. Don't pay for car or truck repairs when you can avoid doing so. This is a notorious way in which people get ripped off. Instead, get assistance from a friend or do minor vehicle repairs yourself whenever possible.

211. Renew your vehicle registration for more than one year at a time if this option is available and offers savings on a "per year" basis. Naturally, you shouldn't renew for more than the length of time you expect to have the vehicle.

212. Consider raising the deductibles on any car insurance that you have, so that you can pay lower premiums. As with several other ideas listed here, this one involves the level of comfort that you have taking risks. **Remember, each of these ideas is only a suggestion, and not every idea is right for every reader. Do what seems right for you.**

213. If you or your family has a "good car" and an older, less valuable car, consider using the older car for most routine trips, any trip that might involve sitting in traffic, and "heavy duty" uses like hauling lawn and garden items, helping someone move, or picking up heavy items. Save the good car for special occasions and thereby preserve its useful life and resale value. Put most of the wear and tear on the older car.

214. <u>Some insurance companies offer a discount to drivers who will attend a driving safety course</u> or who have already done so. These courses are usually inexpensive and relatively brief, and can offer considerable savings over time. If you've already had a driving safety course, you'll want to tell your insurance agent so that you can get any discount they offer.

215. If you don't already know how to do oil changes on vehicles, consider learning to do so as long as you have an appropriate place to perform the work. <u>Also, be sure to do oil changes (or have them done by others) on your vehicle(s) regularly</u>. The cost of replacing a engine is extremely high compared to the cost of routine maintenance.

216. Don't confuse the need for oil changes with the importance of keeping enough oil in your car's crankcase. <u>Add oil whenever your car needs it</u>. The cost of a quart of oil is very low compared to the cost of repairing or replacing an engine. Also, note that performing a simple tune-up and/or replacing your air filter can increase your gas mileage dramatically.

Other / Multiple Topics

217. There is a method of saving 100% on an item. <u>Don't buy it at all</u>. Unless you need something right away, postpone or eliminate the purchase. You might find a less expensive alternative, you might be able to get it for free next week from a neighbor, or you may change your mind about "needing" it.

218. In general, don't pay for service contracts that are sometimes offered when you make a purchase. If an item is worth buying, it should be dependable. (If you are unsure of the dependability of a product, you should consider learning more about it from consumer magazines, some of which are available in local libraries where you can read them at no cost.) Also, try to use the services of a friend or relative when an item is worth repairing and you're not able to do the repairs yourself.

219. Avoid using plastic wrap to cover items in your microwave. When it's practical to do so, use a plate instead of plastic wrap to cover the food. Then, simply rinse off the plate.

220. <u>Try not to pay delivery charges</u>. Especially on local purchases, see if you can work out a way of getting items home by yourself or with a friend's help.

221. For any type of drink that you add ice cubes to, consider adding a bit more ice each time until you find the maximum amount of ice that "works" for you. Ice is nearly free if you make your own. Adding more ice will allow you to spend less, and likely to do so without feeling like you're giving up anything. (All of this is assuming that you have a refrigerator/freezer that allows you to make ice at home rather than buying it by the bag.)

222. If you have children, try to show them how to <u>have</u>

fun with simple things, so that you can reduce your purchases of expensive toys. Kids often get tired of store-bought toys quickly, anyway. If you don't do it already, *you too* might learn to have fun in simple and inexpensive ways.

223. Borrow things. Naturally, you'll want to return items according to your agreement with the lender, but you shouldn't hesitate to borrow things. This can save you a lot of money in the long run, and most people enjoy helping out friends and neighbors, especially if they can borrow from you occasionally.

224. Instead of paying to advertise an item that you have for sale, use one or more community resources. These can include resources such as a bulletin board at a grocery store or a community/condominium newsletter. Free listings on the internet are often a great choice too, especially if they will reach local readers.

225. <u>When you're not satisfied with an item, return it</u> for a refund or exchange. You shouldn't be hesitant or embarrassed about returning an item that didn't meet your expectations or the claims made by its manufacturer. Good stores routinely accept returns, and they do so without any "fuss," especially if you can show your receipt and you are prompt in returning the item. With clothing, returning items that don't fit is a commonly accepted practice in many places. When received as a gift, many people believe it is also acceptable to return clothing that is the "wrong" color or style.

226. Gifts that you don't like can be given to someone else. (But you might not want to volunteer to tell the original giver about this "re-giving.")

227. Try to <u>derive pleasure from simple things</u>. Instead of paying to see a movie, go to a park, play cards, or toss a football, Frisbee, etc. Also, if you want to see a movie, consider renting it instead of paying "per-person" at a theater.

228. <u>Avoid "stupid" expenses</u>. If for example, you drive to visit a friend, be sure you park in a legal space. Many people end up having their car towed at their expense because they fail to ask about parking rules. In short, if you have the feeling that "this could cost me if I don't do what I should"... *then do what you should.*

229. Consider creating a money-savers' club in your area, or joining an existing one. Members can exchange coupons and information on specific bargains, as well as share general advice on saving money.

230. Decorate using a little paint and some creativity. This can reduce or eliminate the need to buy decorative items. For example, paint and stencils can add accents to your kitchen. Stencils are available in various shapes and sizes at many craft stores and "home center" stores. Note: If you rent your home, remember that you might need your landlord's permission before changing the decor.

231. If you like a product or service enough that you are sure to continue using it, try to <u>get a long-term deal</u>. For example, renew the subscription to your favorite magazine for three years (if the per-year rate is lower), instead of paying the single-year rate repeatedly.

232. Leave at least one outdoor light on at night. A few cents worth of electricity is a bargain in this instance, as it will help prevent break-ins and other crimes, and reduces the chance of anyone stumbling in the dark and being injured while on your property.

233. <u>Consider the motives</u> of anyone who tries to sell you something. This doesn't mean that you should necessarily distrust them, but take at least a few moments to consider their motives. For example, are they trying to: sell you something quickly, sell you something that's too expensive, or develop a long-term customer relationship that will be of benefit to them and to you.

234. If you need to get a package to someone, drop it off yourself instead of paying to send it by mail or a delivery service, especially if you can drop off the package during your usual travel. When you *do* pay for delivery, it's usually by weight, so use the most lightweight packaging that's appropriate.

235. When sending mail, you can <u>re-use boxes and large envelopes</u> that you've received. Just completely cross out any writing that doesn't apply and attach a new label. Be sure that any "canceled" postage is removed or completely covered before adding your own postage.

236. <u>Consider paying bills two months at a time</u> when you can. You might even want to pay some bills less often if it's feasible for you – in many cases, you would need to check with the vendor for their policies on such payments. Just be sure that paying less frequently won't incur any fees like late charges or administrative fees. You'll save postage, envelopes, time, etc. **Some people, once their overall finances are in good condition, periodically make additional payments on their mortgage.** With many types of mortgage loans, this practice can *dramatically reduce the total interest paid over the life of the mortgage, and, if practiced consistently, will significantly reduce the amount of time it takes to pay it off.* This is because of the effect of compound interest, and because, at least in the United States, interest must be charged only on the amount you still owe.

237. <u>Make your own buying decisions</u>. This is a good general rule that leads to several major money-saving opportunities. Instead of blindly believing in rumors, hype or advertisements, it's important to <u>learn to gather your own information</u> and make your own wise comparisons before you buy, especially on any major product or service. Your selection can then be based on your own thorough research and/or information from people and organizations that you trust. Also, <u>avoid buying from phone solicitors</u> because often you can find a better deal by checking the internet or a phone book, and sometimes making a few phone calls. **Unless you want whatever a telemarketer is selling, it's very often a waste of your time to listen to their pitch.**

238. It's wonderful to give gifts that help to show people how much you care about them, but this doesn't necessarily mean you have to spend a lot of money. This idea may seem crass, but trying to honor a friendship by spending an extraordinary amount of money *really is crass*. Try to buy gifts that are reasonable in cost, but are not extravagant. Instead of resorting to extravagance, try to match the gift to the person. For example, buy a plant for a plant lover or a coin for a coin collector.

239. If you own vacation property, <u>consider renting out your property</u> for all or part of the year to responsible people whom you trust. This can be very rewarding financially, as it involves extra income and possible tax savings. Also, it's an example of making sure you <u>don't let an asset go unused if you can earn money with it</u>. **However, be aware that renting out real estate involves some record keeping, along with your doing repairs and maintenance or at least supervising these tasks.**

240. <u>Do your own research using consumer guides/magazines</u> before making any major purchase. Consider how well the item meets your needs, the price, and how reliable the product seems to be.

241. You might want to share information that relates to lighting and other safety issues with some of your neighbors. Reduced crime and fewer injuries due to falls should eventually lead to lower taxes and insurance rates for everyone! Also, property values can be are affected dramatically by crime rates in a neighborhood, and a well-lit neighborhood is a sign that the people who live there care about themselves and each other. **Five minutes having a friendly chat with neighbors about safety and security could "pay off" very well over time.**

242. <u>Try not to think in terms of price only</u>. Consider value in terms of reliability and how well an item meets your wants or needs. In other words: a ten-dollar item that lasts for a year is a better value than a two-dollar item that is broken soon after you buy it; and an olive fork, no matter how inexpensive, is of little or no use if you don't eat olives.

243. For minor ailments, <u>consider simple home remedies</u>, **but be sure to see a doctor whenever a condition might be serious or if the symptoms persist.**

244. <u>Trust people, but be willing to look in to things you see or hear</u>. In other words, treat merchants with a certain degree of trust, but "keep your eyes open" for anything suspicious or out of the ordinary. Consider what you read (or hear from others) about them, and then verify the facts for yourself!

245. Before doing errands, <u>make a list</u> of things you plan to do *before you leave the house*. This should reduce the number of trips you make, so you'll save time and save money on gasoline and/or other transportation expenses.

246. <u>Don't pay for storage</u> if you can avoid doing so. Instead, consider asking a friend, relative or neighbor who has some extra space available to let you store items temporarily (also, see "yard sales" in the index). They can be an excellent way to make money as you remove unused items and "clutter" from your home. (Of course, what's considered "clutter" by one person might be "nic-nacs" to another.) There are other options when you can't find a new use for an item. Fix it if it's broken, paint it if it looks old, convert it to a new use, sell it, or give it to a friend who has different tastes or needs.

247. Try to "keep your options open." Don't commit to spending money to solve a problem or to fill a need before you've checked out free or low-cost possibilities.

248. Before the holiday season, you might want to buy batteries at a discount store. On Christmas day, for example, batteries will be difficult to find except at the few, usually higher-priced stores that are open on December 25th.

249. There is some truth to the adage, "Time is money." Whenever you can use a technique that helps you save time, you can then devote some of that time to money-saving tasks like collecting/organizing coupons or comparing prices.

250. If a deal seems too good to be true, you should almost always pass it up; you should at least get more information before any purchase. To paraphrase P. T. Barnum, there are a lot of "suckers" in this world. Try not to be one of them by falling for these "too good" deals.

251. Occasionally, try to look at any money difficulties you might have from a "fresh perspective." In other words, if you have a nagging financial problem of some kind, try to look at it in a new way. As an example, if you have trouble paying your housing costs, it's possible that: (1) you have a spare room that's rentable, (2) you could afford your housing costs if your utility bills were lower, or (3) you simply can't afford to live where you're living.

252. <u>Try not to rent things that you can borrow</u>. Have you ever rented, for example, a CD or DVD, and found out soon afterward that a friend could have, at no cost to you, loaned you a copy of the same music or movie? When having a car repaired, some people have rented a car when a free "loaner" car was available from the repair shop or from an insurance company that was paying for the repairs. Books, tools and ladders, among many other items, also can be borrowed in many cases instead of being purchased.

253. In many rural areas, free or reduced-cost services and/or products are provided through the County Extension Service. Make use of this option when it is inexpensive and meets your needs.

254. <u>Be very careful about any agreement that you might sign</u>. Always be sure to read and understand the document even if you need help from someone in order to understand it. Legitimate business people will wait patiently while you read. Anyone who becomes impatient while you read or pressures you to sign something should be avoided.

In addition, insist on having your own copy of any document that you sign. This is good in case you have a question about it later, or in case you need to assert any rights that you have. Also, many documents that you sign might be needed later for tax or other purposes. It's just a good habit to keep a copy for yourself. Anyone who hesitates to let you have your copy is likely someone you should not do business with.

255. Take advantage of "free offers." However, watch out for anything that seems like such a good deal that it just doesn't feel right. Many offers contain costs or other obligations that may not be made clear to you. Pass up any obligation that you don't need, unless you have a very good reason for accepting the obligation.

256. Set aside a place in or around your home to store "yard sale" items until you're ready to have a yard sale. Then, when the sale date arrives, you won't lose or forget about items you intended to sell.

257. <u>Try to be prepared</u> for unexpected events, like losing your keys. For example, consider giving a set of your keys to someone you trust and carrying their name, address and phone numbers with you. If you lose your keys or get locked out of your house or car, you might save a lot by not having to pay for a locksmith, a tow truck, etc.

258. When preparing items for a yard sale, paint some of the items that you plan to sell, as appropriate. (Spray-painting is quick and fairly inexpensive.) For a few cents per item, you can increase their appearance dramatically. At least wash, polish and/or repair the items.

259. You might want to use the mute button when a commercial appears on TV, if you don't already. This will reduce the number of ads that you're exposed to, which in turn, may help to reduce your purchases of products that you might not need.

260. <u>Certain types of stores offer discounts rates for children and/or a lower price for senior citizens</u>. This can apply to services as well as products. Keep your eyes open for these offers.

261. Check with local radio stations to see if they offer coupons that help local merchants reach new customers. Sometimes this type of coupon will provide a large discount, especially for first-time customers who visit a given vendor. Be aware however, that if you agree to receive coupons by mail, you may receive other promotional material from the station (and sometimes other sources) that you might not want. Only you can decide how much unsolicited mail you're willing to accept in order to obtain discounts.

262. To find quick and easy ways to save some money, keep track of every purchase you make for one week. For that single week, save every receipt and use a notebook to keep track of any purchases for which you didn't receive a receipt. At the end of the week, look over the information you've collected, which is often surprising because people tend to underestimate how much they spend on small, repeated expenditures. For example, you might discover that you've been buying twice as many cups of coffee or cans of soda than you would have estimated. When you've truly looked at the reality of your out-of-pocket expenses, it's much easier to find a few that you can reduce or eliminate.

263. <u>Watch for "freebies" that some companies offer</u>, and take advantage of these free items if they suit your needs. (Note that some companies restrict these offers in some way, often limiting them to first-time customers.) If you have internet access, you might want to search on the name of your town or city, combined with the name of your state and a term like "freebies" or "discounts". Also, you could add to your search a category using a word like "food" or "hardware" to narrow down your search. So, a search might look like this: "Elkhart Indiana freebies hardware". Experiment with combinations of words until you find savings, free offers and/or less expensive suppliers for items that you buy.

264. Remember that for many kinds of products and services, various discounts are available, but only if you ask for the discount! In some cases, you need to meet some condition such as being over a certain age or belonging to an organization such as an automobile owner's association.

265. This tip will seem silly to some people, but could work wonders for others who have trouble building up a savings account. Some people like to have a "trick yourself into savings" plan. What this involves is setting some simple rule for putting money into an interest-bearing account. Usually, the money is placed into a jar (or other container) until it has accumulated for a few days or weeks. Examples include having to set aside $2.00 (into the container) every time you eat in a restaurant, contributing an exact percentage of every paycheck, or putting in every five-dollar bill that you receive back in change from merchants. If you decide to do this, be sure to keep your container in a safe place.

266. Some people make purchases, not because they have a true need, or even something they really want, but because they're bored or they feel that they're under too much stress. Don't be one of these people. Stated another way, don't think of a mall or a shopping center as being primarily a place to have fun. Unless you're very self-disciplined about your spending, get what you need and then leave! Find other forms of entertainment that involve little or no cost.

267. To find coupons, there's another technique you can use in addition to using internet searches mentioned previously. Use internet-based coupon sites to find bargains. They're easy to find using a simple web search on the words, "coupon sites". A few examples are:

Coupons.com

CouponMountain.com

OnlineCoupons.com

DealSeekingMom.com

CouponCravings.com

268. Periodically, think about any clubs that you pay to belong to and consider whether the benefits of a given club are worth what you pay in dues and/or membership fees. You'll probably want to cancel membership, of course, in clubs that don't meet this test. The term "clubs" might include any warehouse-style store that requires a membership, a country club membership, your membership at a gym, and/or social clubs.

269. When you cook food in an oven, it's easy to also wrap a few potatoes in aluminum foil and place them alongside whatever else that you're cooking. After a few minutes, you'll have, of course, baked potatoes – some that you can eat right away, and some that you can refrigerate for later. You'll save on energy costs by not heating the oven twice, and you'll save time too.

270. Try this exercise: ask yourself what single item is one on which you might spend too much money. The first product that occurs to you is very likely something you could buy less of and therefore save money on.

271. When you plan to visit retailer(s) to make a purchase involving a significant cost, make at least one visit before you buy which will be purely an "information-gathering trip." As an example, if you plan to buy a bicycle, go to at least one bike shop. Try out and compare several bicycles, talk to one or more staff members to see if they have a customer-friendly attitude. You can also be honest with the staff, telling them that your visit is an initial information-gathering visit, especially if they begin an unwanted sales pitch.

272. Consider using online "freecycle" websites. These are sites where users give away and/or exchange items that might have otherwise been discarded as trash. Some would say, "One person's trash is another person's treasure," so don't assume everything that's available through these sites is in bad condition; some might simply be unsuited to a particular person's needs. (As with all online resources, be very careful about giving out personal information at these sites, and for any face-to-face meetings, meet only in a public place where there are plenty of other people around.) You can find sites by searching online for the keyword "freecycle" followed by the name of your city or region. Also, there is a "parent" site, **http://www.freecycle.org**, that can help you find local groups and additional information.

273. Once or twice each year, look back at about the last five recurring bills that you've paid. They're usually items like utilities, grocery purchases, and rent or mortgage payments – whatever you tend to pay for very often. (If you've paid by check, look in your checkbook. Otherwise, you should have your copies of money orders, direct payments from credit/debit cards, cash receipts, etc.) Then, make a simple list of those you've paid, starting with the item that normally costs the most money.

The next step can be done over the course of a few days or even a couple of weeks. Working down the list, consider for each bill whether there's a way you might save some money... if there is, then call or visit the seller/provider. Examples: (1) With a mortgage payment, some people can get their lender to drop the charge for private mortgage insurance (PMI), and some people are in a position where refinancing makes sense. (2) A phone bill might contain charges for services (or a package of services) that you might not be using such as "Caller-ID" or a voice-mail box. It might include a higher monthly charge for a calling plan that includes free calls to countries you don't make calls to. (3) Your electric bill or gas bill is a good place to start when considering your energy expenses. If you're paying a lot more than your neighbors, you might want to add insulation to your home. Consider whether you are paying extra for any special features or for a "level payment plan" that you might not need. (4) Note for each bill whether or not you owed interest or other fees because you were late in paying the previous bill... you can't fix what you're not aware of, and companies sometimes make charges like these somewhat hard to find on their bills.

If you're in doubt about whether you can save money on a given bill, you might want to call the seller anyway, just to be sure. You can expect them to try to sell you additional products/services, and therefore, you might need to be insistent about the reason you called so that the conversation stays on the topic of saving money rather than on spending more!

For more information about the author, please visit:

http://www.edcreager.blogspot.com

… and please take a look at other publications and discounts that are available through the website.

Index

Topic	Idea Number
adapting	112
admission tickets	157
advertising	29, 44, 237
air conditioning	
see: utility bills, heating and cooling	
air fresheners	110
air in tires (keeping enough)	207
air vents (in unused rooms)	176
apartment	142, 144, 182
appliances, "fighting each other"	174, 177
appliances, dishwasher	125
appliances, heating & cooling	175 - 177, 193, 194, 200, 203
see also: reducing costs, insulating	
appliances, lawn mower	92
appliances, turn off when unused	188
appliances, water heater	180
arts and crafts	108
attic fan	194
automatic teller machine (ATM) cards	9
automobiles	
see also: transportation	

automobiles, gasoline	24, 159, 164, 245
automobiles, insurance	162, 206, 212, 214
automobiles, registration of	211
automobiles, repairs/maintenance	205, 207, 210, 216, 252
automobiles, safety on the road	162
automobiles, speed that saves gasoline	161
automobiles, tune-ups	205, 216
automobiles, used (buying)	208
bags, plastic (re-using)	72, 133
baked potatoes (cooking alongside other items)	269
baked potatoes (leave skin on)	51
baking soda	99, 109
bananas	41, 56, 63
bank accounts	7, 8, 15, 18
bank "ATM" machines	9
bank statements	11, 18
batteries	119, 248
beach (preparing for trip to)	168, 171
beer	75

beverages

   see: specific drink -or-

   see: doing tasks yourself, drinks

bills, direct payments	16
bills, paying two months at a time	236

bills, review of recurring	273
biscuits and cookies (homemade)	40
books	147, 148, 150, 156
see also: information and entertainment	
borrowing (money)	
see: reducing costs, interest	
borrowing things	223
bottles (carbonated drinks in)	64
boxes and envelopes, re-using	235
bread (as a gift)	136
bread (making your own)	71
buses and subways, special passes	160
buses and subways, using	160, 170
business cards (having cards printed)	130
business cards (outdated)	131
buying in large quantities	20, 28, 58, 64, 76, 77, 132
buying on impulse	22
buying simple products	73
buying too much of an item	31
cabbage	82
cabins/campgrounds (for saving while traveling)	163
cable television (or satellite television)	151
"caller ID" on phones	185
cans (carbonated drinks in)	64

car

   see: transportation

changing oil (on vehicles)	215
charges to watch out for on statements	2, 18
checkout lines, items on display	22
checks (buying checks for checking account)	15
cigarettes	23, 37
cleaning (in general)	91, 99, 100, 113, 127
cleaning dishes	125, 190
cleaning, laundry detergents	20, 106, 138

   see also: personal care & household items

cleaning, laundry, using warm or cold water.	181
cleaning, rather than discarding items	104
cleaning, with water	114
clothes, buying	94, 102, 111, 118, 134
clothes, consignment shops and	134
clothes, labeling with name and phone number	123
clothes, returning	225
clothes, washing	181
clubs (review membership periodically)	268
cocoa butter as a moisturizer	140
coffee	37, 48, 53
cola	43, 64, 98, 168

   see also: doing tasks yourself, drinks

collecting (coins, movies, etc.)	135
colleges and schools, costs	152, 153
combining trips	172
commercials	237, 259
community resources, in general	224
community resources, libraries	150, 218
community resources, recycling	133
see also: "freecycle" websites	
compact fluorescent light bulbs	173
conditioner (leaving tiny amount in hair)	103
consignment shops	134
containers	58, 64
containers, recycling	133
contracts, service	218
convenience (avoid paying for)	24, 30
cookies and biscuits (homemade)	40
cooling	
see: utility bills, heating and cooling	
cost sharing	28, 55, 97, 144, 164, 183
county extension service	253
coupons	38, 42, 121, 137, 229, 267
creativity, using	60, 80, 81, 89, 230
credit cards	2 - 5, 11, 17
credit cards, comparing (and annual fees)	3

credit cards, having too many	5
credit cards, eliminating	17
credit cards, monthly payments and balance(s)	4, 5
see also: reducing costs, interest	
credit cards, receipts and statements	11
creme rinse (leaving tiny amount in hair)	103
cups, disposable (avoid)	124
cups, avoid breakable	128
daily expenses	262
deals, " too good to be true" (be wary of)	250
debit cards (as alternative to credit cards)	17
debit cards, receipts and	11
decisions (use of trusted information sources)	10, 237
decorating	230
delivery costs and postage	16, 220, 234, 236
detergent	
see: personal care & household items	
direct deposit & direct payments	16
discounts (age based for children/seniors)	166, 260
discounts (coupons from radio stations)	261
discounts (coupons on the internet)	137, 267
discounts/refunds, sometimes must ask to receive	154, 264
dishes, washing	125, 190
documents, signing	254
doing tasks yourself, delivery	220, 234

doing tasks yourself, drinks	48, 168, 221
doing tasks yourself, food and meals	32, 54, 61, 66 - 68, 72, 167
doing tasks yourself, freezing foods	56, 67, 68, 72, 76
doing tasks yourself, salads	30, 76
doing tasks yourself, tune-ups	205
"don't buy it at all" method of saving	217

drinks

   see: specific drink -or-

   see: doing tasks yourself, drinks

driving safely	162
dues (review club memberships periodically)	268

electricity

   see: utility bills

eliminating costs, bank accounts	8, 15
eliminating costs, planning	34, 168, 171
eliminating costs, returning goods	225
eliminating costs, usefulness/self restraint	14, 26, 88

eliminating costs

   see also: reducing costs

entertainment

   see: information and entertainment

envelopes and boxes, re-using	235
expenses, sharing	28, 55, 97, 144, 164, 183
extension service	253

extra room (in home)	176, 251
fabric softener	120
family (keeping money in family)	1

fan

  see: utility bills

fan, attic	194

  see also: utility bills

fancy packaging (avoid)	78
fast food / restaurants	32, 36, 43, 66, 167
fees (late fees and penalties)	34, 143

  see also: reducing costs, interest

filter, air filter in automobile	216
filter, furnace	96
fish	45

flavorings

  see: hot peppers -or- lemon juice -or-

  soy sauce -or- spices

food

  see specific food -or-

  see: doing tasks yourself, food

free attractions	155, 169
free items (and "freebie" websites)	255, 263, 272
"freecycle" websites	272
freezing foods	56, 67, 68, 72, 76

fruit juices	46
see also: lemon juice	
fruits and vegetables	50, 59, 62, 76
see also: salads and salad ingredients	
fun with simple things	222
games, computer-based (video games)	85, 158
gas (gasoline)	24, 159, 164, 245
gas, speed that saves	161
gas (natural)	
see: utility bills, heating and cooling	
gelatin	86
gifts	6, 136, 225, 226, 238
gravy	35
groceries	
see specific food -or- see: doing tasks yourself, food	
see also: unit pricing -and- coupons	
groceries, planning meals based on sale items	84
grocery shopping (don't go while hungry)	26
grocery store inserts from newspaper, using	52
habits, cigarettes	23, 37
habits, shopping as entertainment	266
haircare (shampoo and shampooing)	20, 106, 170
hair care (watering down shampoo/conditioner)	138
haircuts	115

"hand-me-down" method good for many items	122
hang on to what you have	123
"hard wired" phones, eliminating	204
heating & cooling	175, 176, 177, 193, 194, 200, 201, 203
holidays, saving during	6, 65, 70, 107, 116, 183, 248
home remedies	243
homemade cookies/biscuits	40
hot peppers	81
"hot water heater"	180
hotels, cabins and campgrounds as alternatives to	163
housing costs see also: loans and mortgages	142 - 144, 182, 203, 230, 251
ice	221
impulse buying	22
information and entertainment, books	147, 148, 150, 156
information and entertainment, free attractions	155, 169
information and entertainment, movies/videos	135, 227, 252
information and entertainment, simple pleasures	227
information and entertainment, television	151
information-gathering visits (before buying)	271
insulation	180, 182
internet as free reading material	150
internet as source of recipes	71
internet , coupons and coupon sites on	137, 267

internet, free listings on	224
internet, "freebies" listed on	263
internet, money-saving sites on	139
internet (sometimes available free)	155
jars	
see containers	
juices	46, 47, 98
keeping your options open	247
"land line" phones, eliminating	204
large quantities, buying in	28, 58, 64, 76, 77, 132
late fees and penalties	34, 143
see also: reducing costs, interest	
laundry, detergents	20, 106, 138
see also: personal care & household items	
laundry, using warm or cold water	181
lawn and yard work	92, 213
learning to sew	95
lemon juice	98
see also: juices	
library (learning at)	
see: community resources	
light bulbs	173, 178, 179, 187, 195, 196
light bulbs, compact fluorescent	173

light bulbs, fluorescent	173, 179, 201
light bulbs, low wattage	173, 187, 195
lighting, cost of	
see: utility bills, electricity and lighting	
lighting, to increase safety & security	187, 241
liquid soap, watering down	138
listing amounts spent	262
"loaner" car	252
loans and mortgages, avoiding	2, 5, 13, 14
loans and mortgages, mortgage brokers	146
loans and mortgages, reducing expenses	
see: reducing costs, interest	
loans and mortgages, refinancing	145
see also: loans & mortgages, mortgage brokers	
loans and mortgages, vehicle loans	14
local (or county) extension service	253
long-term deals	231
loss leaders	27, 33
lunches	67, 68
mail, unsolicited ("junk mail")	149
maintenance (vehicle)	205, 207, 210, 215, 216, 252
major savings techniques: coupons	38, 42, 121, 137, 229, 267
major savings techniques: "don't buy it at all" method of saving	217

major savings techniques: listing amounts spent	262
major savings techniques: reducing costs, housing	13, 142 - 146, 204, 236
see also: loans and mortgages	
major savings techniques: reducing costs, interest	3 - 5, 13, 236
see also: refinancing	
major savings techniques: review of recurring bills	273
major savings techniques: "single item exercise"	270
major savings techniques: stocking up	20, 28, 58, 64, 76, 77, 132
major savings techniques: "Three Cs" method of saving money	19
making your own gifts	136
mall (don't visit for entertainment)	266
meals	
see also: doing tasks yourself, food and meals	
meals, planning based on sale items	84
meat and meat products	39, 45, 62, 69, 83
memberships, review periodically	268
mending clothes	95
moisturizer, cocoa butter as	140
moisturizer, watering down	138
money ("time is money" adage)	249
mortgage brokers	146
mortgage payments	142 - 144, 251
see also: loans and mortgages	

motels, cabins and campgrounds as alternatives to	163
motivated sellers	118, 209
movie tickets, in booklets	157
must ask to get discount / refund	154, 264
name and phone number (put on belongings)	123
national parks, savings at U.S.	166

natural gas

   see: utility bills, heating and cooling

noodles	60, 68
oatmeal	54
oil changes (on vehicles)	215, 216
old-fashioned products	86
old "letterhead" paper (re-using)	129

online

   see: internet

open-minded, remaining	112
options (keeping your options open)	247
outdated business cards	131
oven usage, general	174. 177
oven usage, cooking extra items like potatoes	269
over-buying	31
packaging, avoid fancy	78
packing food to reduce costs before traveling	167
parks	55, 157, 166, 169

parks, national	166
pasta, advantages of	21
paychecks, direct deposit of	16
penalties and late fees	34, 143
see also: reducing costs, interest	
peppers, hot	81
personal care & household items, laundry detergent	20, 106, 138, 170
personal care & household items, shampoo	20, 103, 105, 138
personal care & household items, sponges	104, 113, 117
personal care & household items, toothpaste	20, 105, 109
personal care & household items, watering down	138
phone costs	183, 185, 186, 198
pine cones for fresh scent in a room	110
planning	34, 168, 171
plastic bags, re-using	72, 133
plastic flatware	126
plastic wrap (avoiding)	219
pleasures, simple	169, 227
"pop" / "soda pop"	
see: soft drinks	
popcorn	86
postage and delivery costs	16, 220, 234, 236
potatoes (as a simpler side dish)	50
potatoes (cooking alongside other items)	269
potatoes (leave skin on when baking)	51

potatoes (other ideas)	39, 80, 81, 269
presents (gifts)	6, 136, 225, 226 238
price (try not to think only of price)	242
programmable thermostat	203
public transportation, using	170
purchases, delaying	65
quantities (buying in large quantities)	28, 58, 64, 76, 77, 132
radio stations, discount coupons from	261
records, keeping financial records in order	12
recreation, admission tickets for	157
recurring bills (review of)	273
recycling	133

   see also: "freecycle" websites

reducing costs

   see items below -and-
   see also: eliminating costs

reducing costs, "stupid" costs and expenses	228
reducing costs, being creative	60, 80, 81, 89, 230
reducing costs, bills (examining)	151, 197
reducing costs, buying in large quantities	28, 58, 64, 76, 77, 132
reducing costs, by having roommate	28, 97, 144
reducing costs, converting items for new uses	87
reducing costs, coupons	38, 42, 121, 137, 229, 267

reducing costs, delivery charges	220, 234
reducing costs, electricity and lighting	173, 177, 179, 189, 193, 195, 196, 199, 201, 203
see also: appliances	
reducing costs, gasoline	24, 159, 164, 245
reducing costs, housing	13, 142 - 146, 204, 236
see also: loans and mortgages	
reducing costs, insulating	180, 182
reducing costs, interest	3 - 5, 13, 236
see also: refinancing	
reducing costs, late fees and penalties	34, 143
reducing costs, loans and mortgages	2, 4, 5, 13, 14, 145, 146, 236
reducing costs, making an expense list	262
reducing costs, paying for longer time periods	236
reducing costs, roommates	28, 97, 144
reducing costs, sharing and splitting costs	28, 55, 97, 144, 164, 183
reducing costs, store brands	38, 44, 99, 121
reducing costs, telephone, local	183, 185, 186, 198
reducing costs, telephone, long-distance	184, 198
reducing costs, unit pricing	25, 64
reducing unnecessary shopping trips	74
refinancing (home mortgage)	
see: loans and mortgages, refinancing	
registers/air vents (in unused rooms)	176

registering vehicle for multiple years	211
reliability of products	240, 242
remaining open-minded	112
rent	142 - 144, 182, 251
renting out property	239
repairs	91, 218
see also: automobiles, repairs/maintenance	
replacing only part of an item	90
research, consumer guides	29, 218
research, libraries	218
research (use sources without advertising)	29
restaurants / fast food	32, 36, 43, 66, 167
returning goods	225
re-using plastic bags	72, 133
reviewing memberships	268
review of recurring bills	273
rice	60, 68
room, unused	176, 251
roommate	28, 97, 144, 251
routine shopping, three strategies for	52
safe driving	162
salads and salad ingredients	30, 76
sales, loss leaders	27, 33
sales, yard	101, 256, 258
satellite television	151

sauce, soy	79
sauce, tomato	60
saving time	249
schools and colleges (costs)	152, 153
scratch paper	129
seasons, summer	174, 193, 194, 200, 201
seasons, winter	120, 193
self restraint	14, 26, 88
sellers, motivated	118, 209
service contracts	218
services, try to get a long-term deal on	231
sewing and mending	95
shampoo	20, 106, 138, 170
sharing and splitting costs	28, 55, 97, 144, 164, 183
shipping costs	220, 234
shopping (avoid grocery shopping when hungry)	26
shopping (don't use as entertainment)	266
shopping (information-gathering visits before buying)	271
showers and baths	
see: water heater -and- see: water saving techniques	
shutoff valve, use in saving water	190
side dishes	50, 60
simple things, fun with	222

simplest products	73, 86
see also: side dishes	
"single item exercise" for saving money	270
soap, liquid (watering down)	138
soft drinks	43, 64, 98, 168, 221
see also: buying in large quantities	
softener, fabric	120
sources of information (decisions based on trusted)	10
soy sauce	79
spare room	176, 251
speed that saves gasoline	161
spices	60, 81
sponges	104, 113, 117
statements, bank	11, 18
statements, charges to watch for on	2, 18
statements, debit and credit cards	11
staying open-minded	112
stocking up	20, 28, 58, 64, 76, 77, 132
storage	246
store brands	38, 44, 99, 121
"stupid" costs and expenses	228
subways, special passes	160
subways, using	160, 170

summer	174, 193, 194, 200, 201
Sunday newspaper	52
surprise expenses (avoiding)	34, 143, 168, 257
tea	37, 48
telephone, local	183, 185, 186, 198
telephone, long-distance	184, 198
telephone solicitors	237
television (cable or satellite)	151
television commercials	259
thermostat, programmable	203
"Three Cs" method of saving money	19
three strategies for routine shopping	52
tickets, admission	157
"time is money" adage	249
time periods (save by paying for longer periods)	236
time, saving	249
tires (keeping enough air in)	207
tomato sauce	60
" too good to be true" deals (be wary of)	250
toothpaste	20, 105, 109
trading items (using online "freecycle" sites)	272
transportation, bus and subway passes	160
transportation, combining several trips	172
transportation, free attractions	155, 169

transportation, gasoline	24, 159, 164, 245
transportation, packing food to reduce costs	167
transportation, vehicle insurance	162, 206, 212, 214
transportation, vehicle purchases & loans	14, 209
transportation, vehicle registrations	211
transportation, vehicle repairs/maintenance	205, 207, 210, 215, 216, 252
trash (be careful what you throw away)	192
travel (preparing for recreation/vacation trips)	168, 171
travel (savings at U.S. national parks)	166
"trick yourself into savings" plan	265
trust	10, 29, 57, 165, 233, 237, 244
trusted sources	10
tuna fish	45
tune-ups	205, 216
turn off appliances	188
unit pricing	25, 64
universities, costs	152, 153
unnecessary shopping trips, reducing	74
unneeded items, buying	
see: impulse buying	
used books, getting paid for	148
used car (consider instead of new car)	208
used products (saving by purchasing)	85
using creativity	60, 80, 81, 89, 230

using items in a new way	87
utility bills, electricity and lighting	173, 177, 179, 189, 193, 195, 196, 199, 201, 203
see also: appliances	
utility bills, electricity, fan use in summer	194, 200
utility bills, electricity, fewer lights in summer	201
utility bills, eliminating "land line" phones	204
utility bills, heating and cooling	175 - 177, 193, 194, 200, 201, 203
utility bills, insulating your home	180, 182
utility bills, light bulbs, fluorescent	173, 179, 195, 201
utility bills, light bulbs, low wattage	173, 187, 195
utility bills, telephone, local	183, 185, 186, 197, 204
utility bills, telephone, long-distance	184, 198
utility bills, television (cable or satellite)	151
vacation property, renting out	239
vacations (packing food to reduce costs)	167
vacations (preparing for)	167, 168, 171
vacations (savings at U.S. national parks)	166
vanilla wafers	86
vegetables (and fruit)	50, 51, 59, 62, 76
see also: salads and salad ingred.	
vehicles	
see: transportation	

video games	85, 158
vinegar (cleaning with)	99, 100
washing dishes	125, 190
water heater	180
watering down liquid products	138
water-saving techniques	125, 190, 191
wattage (of light bulbs)	173, 187, 195
websites see: internet	
winter	120, 193
world wide web see: internet	
yard sales	101, 256, 258
yard work	92, 213

About the Author

Ed Creager has a degree in the computer field and experience with databases and document preparation. The author has lived in several parts of the United States and travels extensively.

- - -

For more information please visit:

http://www.edcreager.blogspot.com

… and please take a look at the <u>available discounts</u> on this book and other publications by Ed Creager, which include:

The **EasyTerms**$_{TM}$ **guidebooks containing college-level terms and definitions**, to include such subjects as:

* Botany
* Biochemistry
* Biology
* Cell Biology
* Ecology
* Genetics
* Human Anatomy & Physiology
* Microbiology
* Nursing
* Nutrition
* Psychology
* Zoology

Made in the USA
Columbia, SC
20 January 2025